Anthony Grey's books and short ⟨…⟩ into some fifteen language. ⟨…⟩ *Saigon* and *Peking* are cri⟨…⟩ ⟨…⟩pe, the Far East, South Afr⟨…⟩ ⟨…⟩icas. A former foreign correspond⟨…⟩ ⟨…⟩stern Europe and China, he has written e⟨…⟩ ⟨…⟩ate. His first book was an autobiographical accou⟨…⟩ ⟨…⟩e two years that he was held hostage by Red Guards during China's Cultural Revolution. His most recent novel, *Tokyo Bay*, is the first volume of a trilogy illuminating one hundred and fifty years of tortured rivalry between Japan and the West.

Anthony Grey makes documentary films for British television, broadcasts internationally on the BBC World Service, and lives at present in London.

THE GERMAN STRATAGEM

'The tale moves swiftly from first to last.' *Jersey Evening Post*

'A well-plotted tale this . . .' *Southern Evening Echo*

'Anthony Grey's first novel contrasts sharply with his earlier works . . . Good, swashbucking stuff told at a snappy pace!' *Eastern Daily Press*

'With the constant world monetary crises as his inspiration, Anthony Grey has woven the fabric of his East–West espionage tale with threads of great detail and plausibility . . . a fast-moving story.' *The Natal Witness, South Africa*

'Urbane, quick-moving, different, East-versus-West chase-and-flight thriller . . . would make an interesting movie.' *The Province, Canada*

'It has what most crime addicts like: shocks, gunfights and violence . . . Anthony Grey draws on his considerable experience as a newspaperman around the world.' *Christchurch Star, New Zealand*

Also by Anthony Grey

ANTHONY GREY

THE
GERMAN
STRATAGEM

PAN BOOKS

First published 1973 by Michael Joseph as
Some Put Their Trust in Chariots

This edition published 1998 by Pan Books
an imprint of Macmillan Publishers Ltd
25 Eccleston Place, London SW1W 9NF
and Basingstoke

Association companies throughout the world

ISBN 0 330 31195 6

Copyright © Anthony Grey 1973

1 3 5 7 9 8 6 4 2

A CIP catalogue record for this book is available from
the British Library.

Phototypeset by Intype London Ltd
Printed and bound in Great Britain
by Mackays of Chatham plc, Chatham, Kent

For
my dearest sister June,
who is much missed

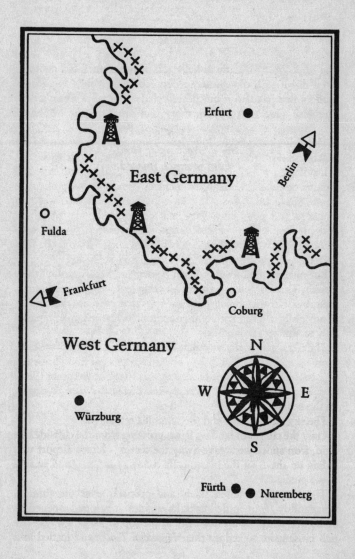

One

The BEA Viscount with its belly full of rich British tax avoiders tilted down towards the steep cliff face half a mile inland. Its shadow fled beneath it on the rumpled water of St Ouen's Bay. The dark shape put a momentary blot on the white ribbon of foam thrown up by the great, surfing rollers.

The airliner and its shadow were closing fast as they crossed the beach and skimmed on over the sandhills heading for the cliff.

Inside the plane, brandy glasses had been drained and collected minutes before. Seat belts were buckled. The distinctive pink pages of the *Financial Times* lying on expensively-clad laps were no longer subject to scrutiny. They had been folded and laid carefully aside. If their owners reached home they would be clipped with scissors or dissected with razor blades. The cuttings would be filed under appropriate headings in share portfolios.

But in these moments the rich passengers had forgotten their wealth. They joined together with their less well-off brethren in the cabin in the unspoken, solemn mass that precedes the landing of any airliner laden with human souls. They hoped and prepared only to survive the landing.

The red wings of the Viscount floated it down towards the cliff. From the beach, land and sky appeared to meet at the silhouetted cliff edge. For an instant land, sky and the Viscount met. With engines roaring the airliner disappeared from the view of people on the beach.

The sky and the cliff and the sandhills remained.

Only the clutter of landing lights growing from the cliffside like rigid, iron sunflowers gave away the secret – Jersey airport was hiding up there on the plateau, its runaway starting and ending at the precipice.

The Viscount, piloted safely and precisely over the stunted, iron sunflowers, throttled back its engines. It stopped, opened its doors and stood its air hostesses at the top of its gangways. The rich passengers picked up their *Financial Times* and jostled in a subdued, well-bred manner in the gangways. The hostesses smiled at them professionally, relieved to see them go. They smiled back, relieved that only the altitude of the airliner's steps now separated them from the ground of the tax haven they called home. And went.

They went in a way that immediately distinguished them from the late summer tourists on the flight – and me.

They strode quickly into the airport buildings. They knew that although Jersey had its own independent government there were no customs for arrivals from London – only from Paris and the Continent. They didn't take up positions with me at the foot of the empty conveyor belt which would bring baggage from the Viscount. They kept straight on and out of the doors to the car park. They didn't have any luggage beyond their slim, black briefcases.

A Lordship's uniformed chauffeur intoned that word with unnecessary volume so that it carried across the forecourt. He obviously enjoyed greeting his master with touched cap and an open Rolls-Royce door. Obedient, soignée, middle-aged wives were waiting for their partners with white, 3.5 litre Rovers and 4.2 automatic Jaguars. The younger men strode by, with a smile and a nod, towards the compound where they had parked their E-types, Ferraris and Alfas that morning.

There had been talk of a society wedding on the plane. Over for the day? Yes, just for the wedding, y'know – and a bit of business.

Now they were back. Where you hang your bank account is home to the mobile rich.

I was still waiting by the empty conveyor belt with the gaggle of tourists as the sleek cars began hurrying off among Jersey's lush hedgerows. They were taking their occupants and their financial newspapers to elegantly converted farmhouses of mellowed granite. Taxes that have eluded the grasp of the Inland Revenue at Somerset House in London have added a rich patina to old Channel Island farmhouses – inside and out.

Among the cars I spotted the face I had been looking for. A tall, thin man with slightly stooped shoulders was picking his way between the vehicles, wearing the bemused expression of someone constantly surprised by the mundane. Even in Berlin where Captain Clarence Smythe had worked as a uniformed spy when I was there, that same bemused expression of one who has never quite understood, was his trade mark.

I smiled in spite of myself. The gap of eight years since Berlin didn't seem so long ago.

He hadn't seen me. He was intent on stepping round the polished carriages of what were probably some of his rich clients. Advocate Clarence Smythe, with a brass plate outside his office in Hill Street, St Helier, now had only the legal and contractual interests of the residents of Jersey at heart.

Or so I thought then.

His head bobbed as he stooped and smiled politely through windscreens, waved and nodded and side-stepped his gangling way across the forecourt. In throwing a last, over-the-shoulder smile at a Dior-clad daughter he failed to see in time a slowly-moving Jaguar. It swerved round him and came to rest up his Lordship's exhaust pipe. A tinkle of glass fell from a headlight.

I stood shaking my head in dumb amusement. Then I stopped.

A stab of half-recognition of another face registered fleetingly. A car had passed in front of Clarence and a head inside turned briefly in my direction to show a face, vaguely and disquietingly familiar.

The car – and the face – was gone an instant before my memory could get a grip on it.

Two

Clarence was stooping his bony shoulders again and waggling his head in profuse apology at the window of the Jaguar. Then he turned and came on, looking more bemused than ever and blushing with embarrassment.

The chauffeur of the Rolls got out to remonstrate with the Jaguar's woman driver. His Lordship, to give him his due, upheld his family's aristocratic traditions by remaining unmoved in the shadowy interior. He sat calmly reading his newspaper until the matter had been settled by those involved. A smashed headlight and bent exhaust were clearly *infra* his *dig*.

'You haven't changed much, you tall, gangling oaf,' I said, holding out a hand and smiling broadly at Clarence.

His firm grip was not consistent with his bumbling progress across the airport forecourt. He grinned from ear to ear.

'These odd little spots of bother do still seem to follow me around, I agree. Anyway, great to see you after all this time. Had a good flight? This your bag?'

He had spotted the leather holdall with my initials, J.R., embossed on the side. His mind and eyes were as sharp as ever inside the clumsy body. He bent forward to pick it up at exactly the same moment as I did. Our heads bumped painfully together.

'Oh, I *am* sorry! Here let me take it.'

I took two exaggerated paces back and motioned him in front with a sweep of my right hand and a bow. Clarence needed lots of room to move; I should have remembered that.

'I see you still carry the journalist's best friend with you,' he said, nodding towards the small portable typewriter I had brought on the plane as hand luggage. 'Still hacking out a living with it, are you?'

'Hacking is right,' I replied, as Clarence opened a taxi door. 'The lot of the freelance journalist is not that of the Jersey advocate. I've heard that a brass plate in Hill Street is a licence to print your own money, is that right?'

'That's a bit vulgar, isn't it?' he said, with mock severity.

Then he smiled. But it was a smile that I fancied was a bit forced, despite his genuine pleasure at seeing me.

'I suppose it's true things haven't gone badly,' he added. 'Plenty of rich mainlanders fled here from the *awful* Harold Wilson in 1968 when they all thought he was going to impose some kind of *dreadful* wealth tax. They've needed a lot of help buying their properties, settling their investments, setting up their companies and trusts. They need a lawyer for all these things, poor dears.'

'I gather I had the privilege of flying here in the same plane with some of them. Doesn't visiting London involve a risk of them getting caught by HM Revenue?'

12

'Not if they're careful. In most cases they can spend ninety days a year in England. A lot of 'em today have been on a day return – which doesn't count at all. You don't count the day you go and the day you return towards your ninety days. So even if you go Tuesday, come back Thursday, you've only spent one day of your ninety legally.'

'How many millionaires have you got now then, snuggling in Jersey's warm embrace?' I asked.

'Old chap, you ask *the* most vulgar questions. Just what you'd expect from a journalist. You haven't changed either.'

Clarence was still good at patronizing condescension. But again I got the impression his heart wasn't in the joke. He stared out of the taxi window and seemed distracted.

I'd almost forgotten my question about millionaires when he said suddenly: 'It's hard to say how many exactly. Between fifty and a hundred wouldn't be a bad guess. A lot of millionaires for an island twelve miles long by five miles wide anyway. Most of 'em are quiet retiring types here, you know, not like the few household names that get themselves into the columns written by your gossip-hungry friends.'

'You mean people like . . .' I mentioned the names of two men who were quietly very rich indeed.

Clarence's eyebrows went up. 'Have you been doing some homework, old chap? Wouldn't have thought you'd have had time.'

'It gets to be a bit of a habit before flying into a new place,' I said airily. 'Even when you've been summoned mysteriously for personal reasons by an urgent cable from a friend. I had a quick chat with a Fleet Street man who does one of the City pages. He said if all the hot money were suddenly taken out of Jersey the island would rise another ten feet out of the sea.'

'Did he?' said Clarence.

'Is that why you sent for me? You want me to help you anchor it down, do you?'

'Your humour hasn't improved much since Berlin, old chap,' Clarence observed drily. 'What've you been doing since then?'

'The whole story's a long story,' I said.

'Be brief,' said Clarence.

'Vietnam in sixty-six, sixty-seven Hong Kong riots, sixty-eight Czechoslovakia, Russian invasion thereof, sixty-nine Biafra, seventy Ulster, seventy-one Bengal. A crisis here, a crisis there. You name it, I wrote it.'

'You always were a modest, self-effacing fellow, I remember now,' said Clarence.

'If you would expand your reading habits beyond the *Financial Times* you might have known that your intrepid reporter friend was constantly risking his life to bring you news from foreign parts with your cornflakes.'

'You're still writing for those vulgar, popular newspapers, then, are you? I had hoped you might one day aspire to the quality dailies. But I might have known.'

We lapsed into silence as we drove down the wooded hill into St Aubin's Bay and turned left along the long sea-front towards St Helier. The evening sun was sending flat shafts of soft, yellow light flooding over the bay. Neatly ranked lines of tomato plants marched up the hillside to the left of the road, reddening in the setting sun.

I was about to question Clarence on his serious-sounding summons when he suddenly spoke, as if reading my thoughts.

'I've booked you into the Grand, just along here on the front. I'm terribly sorry, but I've got to rush straight off to see a client who is waiting at my office now.' He looked quickly at his watch. 'But look, I should be finished by about ten. Have yourself a drink in the bar, and take a leisurely dinner in the Rôtisserie. Tell Sergio, the head waiter, you're my guest and come into town afterwards to meet me at ten o'clock. I'll tell you what it's all about then.'

He gave me directions where to meet him.

As the taxi drew up the ramp in front of the Grand, Clarence turned to me and punched me lightly in the bicep with the side of his fist.

'Look, I'm really glad you've come. I'm going to be able to use your help, I think, in the next day or two.'

The bemused look had quite gone now. But in its place was the intense, drawn look of a man keeping himself under tight control. Perhaps to prevent himself showing he was afraid.

14

Three

The taxi had gone before I was inside the door of the Grand Hotel. A little plaque on the door announced that it rated four stars in the opinion of Jersey's Tourism Committee. In the Rôtisserie Sergio treated me with an exaggerated deference that illustrated Clarence's standing in the island. Lawyers usually have access to local corridors of power – through the side entrances. The head waiter clearly rated him a five-star customer.

While Sergio flourished and flambéd to an accompaniment of Portuguese-accented pleasantries my mind went back to Berlin, the Wall and Captain Smythe's job as a licensed spy in East Germany.

His licence was granted by the Russians – in return for a licence for a Russian officer to spy in West Germany. In uniform and in a military car Clarence drove openly around East Germany, spying as hard as he could go on Russian and East German installations. He was a member of the Military Mission in Potsdam. America and France have missions there too in the same cobbled, tree-lined street where green-uniformed men of East Germany's *Volkspolizei* keep watch from little telephone-box-sized kiosks on the opposite pavement.

Russia's Military Mission is based at Bunde, West Germany, and from there each day uniformed officers drive out to spy as hard as they can go on NATO forces in West Germany. One of the continuing, unpublicized anomalies of Four-Power Control of defeated Nazi Germany. A spy for a spy, a truth for a truth. *Quid pro status quo.*

I arrived in Berlin the night the Wall went up in August 1961. For the next five years I moved under shifty-eyed glances from a multitude of security-obsessed men in and out of uniform, East and West of the Wall. There were more spies to the square yard in Berlin than anywhere else in the world – all incestuously watching one another.

I met Clarence in a tunnel under the Wall.

Small-time crooks made big fortunes in the years following 1961. Bewildered West Berlin families, stunned by the ugly concrete barrier separating them from their East Berlin relatives, willingly parted with their savings to thugs who promised to build tunnels and get their relatives through to freedom. Sometimes they did, but sometimes they just disappeared – with the money.

On one occasion American television men paid one of these *Schleusser* organizations to build a tunnel in which refugees could be filmed 'live' dashing through from the East. It was the British Sector and I was there. The American cameramen got their emotive pictures of scared East Berliners dashing white-faced up the tunnel, blinking in the unexpected glare of the camera lights.

Then the armed East Germans who guarded the Wall discovered the tunnel. It was probably the camera lights.

They came through firing from the East and the escape organized for the nine o'clock news became a mad scramble for safety by the not-so-brave men of the media. Clarence was there to keep a military eye on things. He found himself with the task of trying to get me to my feet when I went sprawling in the mad dash for the Western end of the tunnel. The East German guards came on, firing. He hadn't succeeded when two of them rounded the last corner and came up on us with torches and machine-guns. While they stopped, unsure of how far they had come under the Wall, Clarence pushed me ahead of him and got us back into the main body of the disorderly exodus. My back tingled in anticipation but no further shots were fired. We turned to see a civilian had come up behind the surprised soldiers. He had apparently ordered caution on seeing the British Army uniform. Clarence told me later that he had recognized the senior civilian – a senior SSD man named Hartmann.

I paused suddenly, a consignment of Sergio's finely flambéd steak hovering halfway to its goal. The face of the civilian in the tunnel behind the hesitating soldiers – the face in the car at the airport. Could they have been the same? Hartmann? I let my wrist move the fork on towards its target, trying hard to recall the fleeting moment. But it was spoiling the flavour of Sergio's artistry, so I gave up.

16

I was still mulling over the past in Berlin at ten o'clock while I waited for Clarence, standing in front of the monument at the end of Broad Street, where it becomes a kind of square in the centre of St Helier. The square is bordered by the offices and vaults of the four clearing banks.

The pavements were quiet and deserted. But the bright fluorescent street lights lit up the pseudo-Gothic and wedding-cake Doric façades of the National Westminster, Lloyds, Barclays and the Midland. The top layer of icing on the Midland had a clock in it with its hands at two minutes past ten.

These banks could afford icing. Four hundred and thirty million pounds in bank deposits had poured into the island last year. I'd read that in the *Jersey Evening Post* over coffee and brandy in the hotel lounge. The banks around the square did four times as much business as branches in England. Good for them.

I saw that the street sign for Broad Street had a French subtitle 'La Grande Rue'. A reminder for anybody who forgot that France is only fifteen miles away while England is a hundred. Most of St Helier's streets had subtitles, I noticed.

Not like Clarence to be late. He was renowned for his punctuality in Berlin, and his punctiliousness. The bemused manner melted like meringue on the face of the dessert when he applied his legal mind to a problem.

What monument had he chosen for our rendezvous? I was beginning to think in subtitles now. I turned and gazed up at the plinth that looked like an under-privileged Cleopatra's needle.

It was dedicated to a local worthy of the past.

'This monument was erected by his grateful fellow citizens to Peter La Sueur,' it said. But they didn't say for what they were grateful.

'Born November 20th 1811.'

'Died January 16th 1853.'

Nice and neat. The dates carved on the stone, one under the other, said everything and nothing about his life. Beginning and end. I envied the tidiness. Perhaps because mine was a particularly untidy life.

The wedding cake clock struck ten fifteen. I looked round the quiet square and there was still no sign of Clarence. I walked round the plinth to the side. Behind it was a public lavatory and a globe above the door bore two words 'Gentlemen' and '*Hommes*'. Very useful, no doubt, for a desperate, non-linguist Jersey Frenchman. But the bulb in the globe was gone so it shed no light. I hoped the desperate Jersey Frenchman wouldn't be short-sighted, too.

On the side of the plinth I was able to learn a bit more about Peter Le Sueur – or Pierre Le Sueur as he was now bi-lingually called.

'*Il se devoua au bien-être de son pays.*' Good for him. I went back to the front and round to the other side.

'*Cinq fois élu Connétable de St Helier.*'

Now wasn't that really something? Any man who had been five times *Connétable* – or mayor – was surely worth further investigation, if you had nothing better to do.

What did it say on his back side? I walked round. Normally it would have been lit from the bulb in the Gentlemen-*Hommes* globe but, because it was out, the back of the plinth was in shadow.

I moved up close and stood on my to es to peer at the stone in the gloom.

'*Ses concitoyens reconnaissants . . .*'

The toe of my shoe touched something soft as I leaned forward and I didn't read the rest of the sentence. I looked down.

It was Clarence's face.

He was sprawled in the shadow at the base of the plinth. He'd said he'd be finished about ten. He'd been right. There was a large lump behind his left ear. His licence to print money, if he'd ever had it, had been revoked.

He was dead.

Four

I had seen enough dead bodies in the Pakistan cyclone disaster to last me a lifetime. In Biafra famine and civil war had achieved the same results – except the bodies were black instead of brown. In

18

and out of Vietnam I had seen white and yellow dead – but this doesn't help when close to home you come across the face of a dead friend with your left toe-cap.

I stood and stared down in disbelief. I half expected Clarence to haul himself awkwardly to his feet, apologizing profusely for another bit of bumbling. But he didn't.

My daze was broken by the sound of leather soles shifting quietly across concrete. I looked about the silent street and saw nobody.

Then I spun round, remembering the darkened entrance to the Gentlemen-*Hommes*. I practically blocked the doorway because of the nearness of the obelisk of Peter Le Sueur. The hunched shape of a man moved quickly towards me, knocked me aside. I stumbled back startled, flinging my arms out to regain my balance. By the time I had stabilized myself, the hunched shape had become the figure of a heavily-built man running fast along deserted Broad Street.

The face on that heavily-built body that I glimpsed coming at me out of the darkness of the lavatory was one I had seen twice before. The first time was in a tunnel under the Berlin Wall, the second passing in a taxi at Jersey airport that evening.

But now all I could see was the back of his head – and that was disappearing fast. So I ran too.

As I passed the Central Post Office the East German was some seventy yards ahead. Our feet rang on the pavements of the empty street. A car came slowly from the opposite direction, but it ignored us. I crammed on all the speed I could. But after thirty-six years the human male body doesn't move at its smoothest top speed – especially if the moving parts have been generously lubricated with alcohol and nicotine for eighteen of those years.

The German moved with surprising speed, reflecting the care with which he had trained for his job.

He went out of sight to the left at Charing Cross. When I rounded the corner he was half-way along a dark street that ran between fruit and vegetable warehouses to the sea-front. A car moved out from between two warehouses and pulled across in front of him. He wrenched the door open and flung himself in

19

beside the driver. I slowed to a halt with my lungs heaving. The car gathered speed, swung out on to the Esplanade and turned westwards. Only then did the driver switch on his lights. By that time the car was sideways on to me and I had no chance to see its number.

After a moment I started to run again. Not back to Broad Street but on towards the sea-front. I was heading for the nearest telephone – in my bedroom at the Grand a few hundred yards away.

I slowed to a walk fifty yards before the Grand to recover my breath. The receptionist looked up from painting her nails as I went through the quiet lobby and up the stairs. Dark girl, brown eyes, wide mouth. Nice smile. All inconsequential, but after a few years the reporter's mind can't stop taking mental notes.

I flung off my jacket in the room. I had sweated right through my shirt. What the hell was Hartmann doing in Jersey among late season British holidaymakers and the rich tax avoiders? Why had he killed Clarence? What was Clarence going to tell me? More important, what should I do about it? My reporter's instinct had led me to a telephone. The best story in the world is nothing if you can't communicate it – that's the journalist's maxim. So keep close to your lines of communication. Instinct had taken over. I looked at the white bedside telephone.

The police? Clarence's wife? I had never met her. Clarence had married since Berlin but my first impulse was to think of softening the blow. So, Clarence's wife first, then the police.

I picked up the directory from the bedside table and began looking for Smythe. The sudden ringing of the phone startled me.

'A call for you, Mr Robson,' the brown eyes and wide mouth were telling me from reception.

A guttural voice with the faintest hint of an accent from somewhere in the Balkans came on.

'Mr Robson? You won't know me, but my name is Kerensky. Mr Clarence Smythe, my advocate, told me you had arrived in the island. He knew you in Berlin, I believe . . .'

'That's right,' I said shortly.

'I hope you'll pardon my not waiting for Mr Smythe to introduce us but I know he is a busy man. I am afraid I

20

prevented him from dining with you tonight.' The Balkan-English was carefully apologetic. 'I kept him in his office until nine-thirty. I thought you would be with him now, in fact. I only rang to leave a message for you, when the receptionist told me you were in your room . . .'

'Perhaps it's a good thing you didn't wait for Mr Smythe to introduce us,' I said sharply.

'I'm afraid . . . afraid, I don't understand,' the telephone said.

'Don't you? Well Clarence Smythe won't introduce anybody to anybody again. He's lying dead in Broad Street at this moment,' I said and listened carefully for the response.

I heard the man at the other end of the line suck in his breath sharply. He was silent for a good five seconds.

'Are you sure?' the voice said at last. 'There couldn't be some mistake, could there?'

I thought of my toe against Clarence's face and said, more quietly this time, 'No, there can be no mistake.'

'Dead you say?'

'Murdered,' I said.

'But why?'

'I don't know why – yet.'

'Have you told the police?'

'No, not yet. I was about to call them when you rang.'

Another, longer pause. Then the voice was composed again.

'Mr Robson, may I suggest something? Would you like to come to my house immediately, perhaps spend the night here? And leave calling the police until later? Somebody else will surely inform them.'

'Why?' I asked. I was curt, probably because he was calm and thinking clearly and I wasn't.

'Because Clarence Smythe had asked you here on my behalf and I was going to put a proposition to you that might have interested you. I wanted to ask if you would have been interested in doing a job for me for . . .' the voice hesitated, then went on quietly, 'for a hundred and fifty thousand pounds.'

It was my turn to suck in breath sharply. I wrote stories from datelines all around the world for Fleet Street papers. I didn't do it for nothing. But people didn't offer sums of that magnitude for them – or anything like it.

'Give me your address,' I said. Then I hung up, called a taxi, packed my holdall and dropped that and my portable typewriter out of the balcony window on to the deserted, darkened terrace of the Café de la Paix below.

Five minutes later I sauntered through reception lighting a cigarette. I smiled at the girl with the brown eyes and wide mouth and stepped out into the taxi. I made the driver pull round the corner. There I picked up my bags.

Then we headed out into the dark Jersey countryside.

Five

When the mountains of rock in the Channel hunched their backs many thousands of years ago and pushed upwards they didn't leave much of themselves above the water-line. The dry hump that has become Jersey measures only twelve miles by five. That was practically the first thing Clarence had told me. But on that hump the men of Jersey have traced a fine spider's web network of roads and winding lanes. The garrulous taxi-driver seemed proud of this mania.

'Only twelve by five but we've got over six hundred miles of roads,' he said over his shoulder.

After a few minutes in the taxi I began to think we were going to nose round all six hundred miles to reach Kerensky's house.

We had left behind the sea-front hotels and boarding houses in St Helier and were out among potato and flower farms and the country houses of Jersey's wealthy immigrants. High granite walls of orange stone and white gate-posts showed in the headlamp beams as we swung through narrow lanes roofed over by trees on either side. The fresh night breeze drove the first yellowing tatters of leaves in eddying swirls before the taxi.

A farm worker on a cycle wobbled drunkenly in front of us. The taxi-driver slowed to pass him and the man's voluble swearing in

French penetrated the wound-up windows of the car as he struck the grass bank and fell slowly sideways.

'Not spending his six thousand pounds very wisely is he?' I said to the taxi-driver.

'Beg pardon, sir?'

The driver's Jersey accent made him sound like a South African.

'In your newspaper tonight it said over four hundred million pounds poured into Jersey's banks last year – that's about six thousand pounds for every man, woman and child in the island according to the fellow that drew up the statistics. Our friend on the bicycle – or should I say off it? – seems to have been out trying to spend all of his tonight.'

The driver laughed politely at my wit.

'There's a lot of people 'ere, sir, who've never 'ad as much as that – but quite a few who can't remember when they 'ad as little, ay?'

He nodded towards a long granite wall we had been running along for a minute or two to underline his last point. Jerseymen turn every statement into a question with that little word 'Ay?'

'Of course, sir, you may not know it but the UK belongs to Jersey not vice versa. We were part of Normandy when William the Conqueror went over to you in 1066. You became our colony, ay? We stayed when the rest of France decided to mind its own business again. Lot of people don't know that, ay?'

I laughed politely in my turn.

Behind low walls at the roadside Jersey cows shifted in the darkness on their tethering ropes.

We had reached the western end of the island and descended to the straight road which follows the line of St Ouen's Bay.

There was a whoosh and a roar overhead and red lights skimmed low above the car, jerking me upright in my seat. I had been peering nervously through the rear window during the journey for signs of pursuit. The late-arriving Viscount made me panic momentarily for not having kept a watch overhead.

The plane sank down towards the cliff-face and the airport half a mile inland, as I had done a few hours earlier. It slipped through the slit between land and sky, over the yellow, stunted wallflower landing lights and disappeared, throttling back its engines with a roar.

Between the road and the beach the blunt shoulders of German bunkers were silhouetted against the sea. Built with Teutonic thoroughness during the five-year Nazi occupation of Jersey, they have resisted all peace-time efforts to blow them up.

Then we were turning through hairpin bends and climbing steeply to the high bluff at the end of the bay.

I looked out of the rear window. The tide was out and in the faint moonlight the gnarled and twisted shapes of granite outcrops ran far out into the flat bay. The formless mass of rocks could have been a petrified moment a million years old, when life had just dragged itself shapeless from the sea, groping for form and direction.

I turned back at the sound of the driver cursing and was blinded by a flood of light through the windscreen. We swung over towards the verge.

A long, lighted coach filled with singing holidaymakers squeezed by us on the narrow hill. 'Three Historic Jersey Inns Tour' said a sign that ran past me on the side of the coach at eye level.

Before the driver could pull back on to the road another lumbering, lighted monster was on us, taking home a further sixty singing customers sated with the historic ale of the three inns.

When we got clear of the coaches the driver accelerated away fast.

'Take the gentleman you're visiting, sir.' The taxi-driver was apparently picking up the conversation where he had stopped five minutes before. 'He's got a bit more than his six thousand share. Oh, yes, Mr Kerensky would have considerably more, ay?'

'Like taxi-drivers everywhere you seem well-informed,' I said. 'You'd make good spies.'

The shoulders in front of me shook in a laugh. The smile stayed on the face after the laugh died. The compliment had pleased him.

'We stand around the rank at the airport and exchange gossip, us taxi-drivers,' he said. 'We watch 'em all come and go, ay? It's

24

a small island. Mr Kerensky travels a lot. And his daughter, too. You know Miss Kerensky, sir?'

I said I didn't.

The driver made a sort of smacking noise with his lips, waggled his head, and finished with a long, whistling and humming noise.

'Which means?' I asked, a bit unnecessarily.

'Very attractive, sir, very attractive indeed. You'll see, sir. Yes, I should think Mr Kerensky is worth more than his six thousand share all right.'

He nodded to himself as he contemplated silently the wealth of a man whose backside occasionally graced his taxi.

'Maybe a million or two, he's worth I should think, sir. Jewish, of course.'

We were running alongside a big granite wall. The driver slowed and stopped at a high arch blocked with tall, white solid wood gates. I got out, paid off the taxi and rang the bell. The gate didn't open until the taxi had pulled away.

It was dark inside. Then a whiff of expensive perfume floated out.

'Miss Kerensky?' I said to the shadowy shape inside. 'My name's Robson.'

'Yes. Please come in, my father is waiting for you.'

I stepped carefully through the small wicket gate that made only a small hole in the portcullis-sized entrance. I stepped carefully so as not to upset the two Alsatians that leaned towards me at the end of taut chains, with subterranean growls rumbling from somewhere deep down in their chests.

Six

Inside I saw that the dogs were held by a man standing behind Kerensky's daughter.

'This is Weeks, our gardener. You don't need to worry about the dogs while he's around,' she said.

She led the way across an expanse of immaculately raked gravel to the lighted front door set behind a portico of fluted Doric pillars. I followed, hoping Weeks would always be around.

At the foot of the marble steps two small, stone lions stood guard with trailing plants growing in bowl-shaped crowns on their heads. A rose garden ran round the inside of the high granite walls that enclosed the house and its lawns. Light from the windows splashed the darkness of the enclosure. The walls looked as if they had been built to withstand a siege – which it turned out they had.

I carried my bag and typewriter behind her silhouette; thick, long hair, dark or maybe red, a long dress and a slipstream of a delicate perfume.

George Kerensky was waiting in the hall. His handshake was infirm like the man, although he wasn't really old. Shaggy eyebrows, shrewd, withdrawn eyes, a slight stoop, not very tall. An air of weariness. But when he spoke his words were incisive, suggesting a vigour once greater than now. He announced himself formally and introduced me to his daughter Rodica.

They relieved me of my luggage and led me into a drawing-room that reminded me of one of the small state rooms in the palace at Monaco. That was the only other place I'd ever seen red silk brocade wallpaper. I was motioned to a low chair covered in cordovan leather. The ends of its arms were carved to resemble the paws of a lion. A log fire crackled in the enormous granite fireplace.

'It was a great shock to learn from you that Clarence Smythe was dead,' Kerensky said. He sighed heavily in an agitated way, shook his head and asked: 'Do you know who killed him or why? How did he die?'

I looked at Kerensky, but said nothing. He wasn't the kind of man who won your trust on sight. My silence made him uncomfortable, made him look even less trustworthy. His daughter unlocked the retaining tantalus bar of a set of ornamental cut-crystal decanters and offered whisky.

'Would you like ice or water?' she said.

I looked at her. Her hair *was* red or rather a rich, copper brown. She was taller than her father, suntanned, strong-looking, and the contours of the loose, casually expensive gown gave only a hint of the heavy surge of her breasts.

'Neither, thanks.' I took the glass and gulped a good bit of it down, suddenly realizing how much I needed a drink.

I looked steadily at Kerensky. 'Before I say anything at all I think it's your privilege to answer some of my questions.' A bitter edge came back to my voice of its own accord. I was blaming them for Clarence's death, I suppose.

'I arrive here on the evening plane and three hours later a friend is dead. I know nothing about you. Maybe you had something to do with it. I think you'd better explain where you fit in.'

Kerensky's voice was quiet when at last he found the words he was looking for. He sipped at watered whisky. 'There are many things I don't understand. But you must believe me that Clarence Smythe was my advocate. He and I enjoyed a relationship that was good professionally and went beyond to what I like to think was friendship.'

The Balkan accent had seemed thicker on the phone, perhaps under the stimulus of shock. Faint traces of my own Yorkshire accent, I'd noticed, thickened with passion or pressure. His voice was guttural but he continued without much trace of what I guessed was his native Romanian.

'I think it is possible Clarence Smythe may have died because of my affairs. But before I tell you more about that I must know whether I can trust you. I believe you are a newspaper-man?'

I didn't feel in the mood for making pledges to strangers about my character or my profession – and said so.

'Clarence died before he had the chance to tell me why he asked me to come,' I went on. 'He wanted some kind of help. I don't understand why he didn't go to the police if his life was in danger. I don't really think you have any choice. Perhaps you had just better put your trust in the judgement of a dead man. He had decided I was worth the risk. The choice is yours. I've nothing to lose – or to hide.'

I looked round and saw that Rodica Kerensky was avoiding her father's glance, her eyes cast down to her lap.

His dark eyes narrowed as they inspected me from under the shaggy brows. The looseness of his mouth showed that fear was fighting his mistrust and desire for secrecy.

He shrugged wearily at last. 'All right. I told you on the telephone I had a proposition. I'll tell you as much as I know on the understanding that if you refuse you will respect my confidence.'

I waited and said nothing. I knew he had to tell me anyway now, conditions or no conditions.

He fiddled with the heavy whisky tumbler and stared at the remaining disc of whisky as he spoke.

'You and most people know that Jersey is a tax haven with a standard rate of twenty new pence in the pound income tax . . .'

'Yes, and no capital gains tax, no death duties, we all know that. That's why people with fortunes worth protecting come here from England to live. You can spare me the lecture on Jersey's fiscal laws.'

He ignored the deliberate rudeness and continued, still staring at his whisky.

'What is not so well known is that Jersey is a repository for money from all over the world sent here by people who don't live in the island and may never come here in their lives.'

'Hot money, funk money, you mean,' I said.

'Different people call it different things,' he replied evenly, keeping his eyes averted. 'It's money that's following the best interest rates of the day on the international money market. It comes, it goes, no tax is paid here on it. Above all it's money looking for a safe home, political stability . . .'

Rodica Kerensky took my glass and refilled it, adding some ice this time, at my request. I watched her walk back across the room, noticing that the toe-nails inside her gold sandals were painted a pale shade of pink. I noticed this because my chair was very low. When I turned my head my gaze was at a level below her waist. As she walked towards me the knees and thighs of her long legs rumpled the lines of her gown, were shaped for an instant by the fall of cloth, retreated, then were outlined again. I expect I stared. I was glad when she sat down again and was still.

'What you're getting round to telling me is how you work your own particular fiddle, I suppose,' I said to Kerensky.

I saw him take a deep breath, glance at his daughter. She shot him a thin smile of encouragement.

'I'm sorry you feel obliged to be rude . . .' he said gently.

'You didn't stick your toe in Clarence's dead face,' I cut in. 'If it weren't for your sophisticated financial three-card tricks he might be alive. And God knows it must be something special to bring Communist agents swooping down on the island.'

He stiffened in his chair and I could feel his daughter staring too.

In the silence that followed I heard a shoe scuff the tiled floor outside the door leading to the hall. I turned in my chair. I remembered the sound of feet shifting in the darkness of the 'Gentlemen-*Hommes*'. As the door handle twisted I leapt to my feet and faced the doorway.

The eyes of Kerensky and his daughter widened further. They stared at me – and a Portuguese manservant who came in with a tray bearing a fresh bucket of ice, a jug of water and lemon slices, stared too.

Seven

I turned a sheepish face back to them. Conscious of the fact that I looked about four feet six inches tall instead of six feet four, I sat down again and continued to look foolish for several seconds more.

'We have two Portuguese working in the house, Fernando and his wife,' Rodica Kerensky said through a quietly amused smile. 'There are quite a lot of Portuguese working in hotels and private houses. They come here mainly from Madeira.'

I was grateful for that smattering of astutely-timed cocktail party talk. It allowed me to fix my look of dignity back in place. Fernando went out, closing the door quietly behind him.

'It's been a night of surprises,' I mumbled. I picked up my drink and waited for Kerensky to resume his explanation.

'I think you can feel quite safe here.' Kerensky was talking again through a small cloud of blue smoke from a short Dutch cigar he had just lit. My discomfiture had helped his composure. 'This is a fortified farmhouse,' he said.

'Fortified against whom?' I asked, paying careful attention to my grammar.

'Pirates, in the first instance. This house was built in the sixteenth century. Jersey was a crossroads over which the French and the English trampled in their endless wars. And when national armies weren't pillaging, pirates dropped in to ravage the island and stock their ships with grain. The peasants didn't like this. There are a number of these small farm fortresses dotted through the island.'

'And now you've got modern defences, too, in Weeks and the dogs,' I said sarcastically.

'We also have electrified wires on top of the walls. Farmers here fence their fields with single-strand electric wires to keep the cows in. Our charge is, of course, a bit stronger.'

The lines of his sallow face suddenly all pointed up towards his ears in an approximation of a smile.

'You were explaining big financial swindles . . .' I reminded him, 'and how Clarence got himself killed.'

The muscles in Kerensky's jaw tensed. He was probably gritting his teeth.

'Jersey's big attraction is its political stability,' he went on, studying the end of his cigar. 'There are no party politics here. It has an old-fashioned, partly feudal, attachment to good order. Money has been flowing in from places like the Caribbean, Malta and Singapore in the past year in greater quantities than ever before, because these areas lack that stability. It's likely to continue. Jersey is becoming increasingly significant as a world financial centre – in a quiet, self-effacing way.'

'Look, what has all this stuff about the Gnomes of Jersey got to do . . .' I began.

'Money,' he said ignoring the interruption, 'that comes to Jersey from abroad in the form of foreign currency has as much flexibility here as it has say in Switzerland or Hong Kong. The money over which I have part control is this kind of money. And it was in the administration of this that Clarence Smythe was concerned.'

'How much money is involved?' I put in bluntly. Mentally I heard Clarence chiding me wearily about my *vulgar* questions.

There was the kind of brittle, uncomfortable silence that always follows a straight question to a rich man about his own personal wealth.

Kerensky had probably spent his life playing his cards close to his chest where his money was concerned. Now he had to reveal all to a belligerent stranger, because a fist of fear was tightening its grip somewhere inside him.

'It is a complex matter,' he said at last.

I took a cigarette from an inlaid box on the low table of Venetian marble beside my chair, and waited.

He put down his drink and cigar, placed his elbows on the arms of his chair and rested his two thumbs against his eyebrows. He spoke downwards into the space between his wrists and elbows.

'I am now the senior member of my family and our money is held in a joint trust.' His voice was a bit muffled as if he could hardly bear to tell. 'I have two brothers. One lives in Switzerland, the other in France at Avignon. We constitute the members of the Trust.'

The next pause was so long that finally I prompted. 'That doesn't sound a problem in itself. There are laws governing trusts. You presumably have a framework of legal protection.'

'This is not an ordinary trust,' he said quickly, raising his head to look at me. 'Our Trust is not officially resident anywhere in the world. It is not subject to the laws of any one country and the funds are often on the move – Luxembourg, Liechtenstein, the Bahamas, Malta, Hong Kong and so on.'

'And Jersey,' I added heavily.

'Yes, and Jersey. But because the Trust is not rooted anywhere, it has no direct legal protection, it has no recourse to litigation, cannot sue or be sued.'

'I begin to see,' I said, sitting back in my chair. 'And I suppose no tax is paid anywhere in the world?'

'Not directly on the Trust funds, no.' Kerensky's head was back resting between his thumbs. 'But a reduced amount is paid in different places by us trustees in our private capacities.'

Kerensky was silent again. I could see I was going to have to ask more. Kerensky could not bear to betray himself voluntarily.

'What funds does the Trust now have? What kind of figures are we talking about?'

The answer finally came after another long silence in which I listened to the occasional snap of the burning logs. And then Kerensky's voice was close to a whisper.

'Twenty-five million pounds.'

Kerensky had straightened the fingers of his hands until they were flat together. His head remained bowed over his thumbs. I thought for a moment that he was praying.

'Twenty-five million pounds,' I said slowly, 'no legal protection, no tax anywhere in the world – sorry, a reduced amount – and your only real security, secrecy, has been blown somewhere. Now greedy claws are into you in some way and you've nowhere to turn to the forces of law and order for protection.'

I shook my head trying to take it in. But one thing was still puzzling me.

'If your Trust is not registered anywhere in the world, how is it administered? Surely there has to be a meeting of the trustees to carry out the provisions of the Trust. Surely you have to meet on the soil of some country? And doesn't that make you liable to pay tax here? And if you come clean wouldn't it entitle you to some police protection?'

I looked from Kerensky to his daughter who was turning her whisky glass slowly in her lap, studying each movement intently. Only the shivering of the large pendant ear-rings she wore gave away a hint of tension.

'The Trust meets once a year according to its settlement deeds – but not in any country.'

The words had a resigned note and I turned back to look at Kerensky, who had uttered them. He was still addressing the space between his elbows.

'What do you mean "not in any country"? Do you hire a rocket from Cape Kennedy and go to the moon to read the minutes?'

Nobody seemed to be in a mood to appreciate my joke. Then I found it wasn't much of a joke.

After another heavy silence Kerensky looked up at me with a strangely defenceless expression on his sallow face.

'The Trust meets in an aeroplane that flies from Jersey Airport out into the Atlantic. The meeting takes place outside any territorial waters. All the meetings for the past twelve years have been held in aeroplanes.'

'Oh, hell,' I said and sank further down in my chair. 'We've got the secret AGM flying around over the Atlantic disposing of twenty-five million pounds, harried by East German agents aiming to bring off the biggest bank robbery in history. Oh hell.' I reached for my glass, drained it and voiced the logical conclusion. 'And you want Jonathan Robson to play the cops opposite East Germany's Communist robbers – for a hundred and fifty thousand pounds. And all in secret.'

Nobody answered. I looked at Kerensky and then his daughter. But neither of them was looking at me.

'One last thing,' I said, 'when *is* the next meeting?'

'A charter aircraft will be standing by at Jersey Airport on Monday morning,' said Kerensky. 'It's the latest possible date.'

The Hohenzollern antique clock on a table beside the fireplace chimed midnight, its innards swinging and clicking visibly inside its glass case. The first minute of Saturday morning ticked by silently without a word being said. A splutter of sparks danced on a log then was sucked up the cavernous chimney.

'"Some put their trust in chariots and some in horses, but we will remember the name of the Lord our God",' I said.

Kerensky and his daughter looked towards me with puzzled frowns.

'I beg your pardon?' he said.

'I went to one of those schools where you had to learn and recite long passages from the Psalms as punishment for bad behaviour . . . so I learned a lot of Psalms. The line I've just quoted is from Psalm number twenty.'

They still looked nonplussed.

'This stunt of yours is a very old trick, you see. Your ancestors were doing it back in the wilderness – and getting into trouble even then.' I closed my eyes to recall the words.

' "Some put their trust in chariots . . ." ' I opened my eyes again. I'd remembered.

Kerensky shifted uncomfortably in his seat and his daughter's face darkened in anger. But she said nothing.

'Do you remember the next line?' I asked. 'About those who put their trust in chariots, *not* in the name of the Lord?'

Nobody spoke so I quoted again.

' "They are brought down and fallen; but *we* are risen and stand upright." '

I took another pull at my drink. Setting the empty glass down carefully on the table I said, almost to myself: '. . . and some put their Trust in aeroplanes . . .'

Eight

To break an awkward silence I asked Miss Kerensky if I might have another drink, please. I think I asked as much to see her knees and thighs rustling the gown towards me again, as for my thirst's sake. She leaned over and put the whisky on the side table. Copper-brown hair fell forward to hide her face. Her delicate perfume lingered for a moment longer than she did, then followed her demurely back to her chair. My eyes were able to enjoy only half the journey because Kerensky was sitting upright again asking questions.

'Would you tell us now what happened to Clarence Smythe?'

I did, leaving nothing out. I said I knew the face of the East German who rushed at me out of the darkness and that he had at least one accomplice in the car.

'So they have come to Jersey,' Kerensky said. Fear was carving the lines of age deeper into his face.

'Look,' I said. 'What exactly do you think they intend to do and – what's more important to me – what did Clarence and you think I might be able to do that would stop them? I don't spend my life going round taking on whole phalanxes of Communist agents single-handed.'

'Clarence said you knew Berlin – and the East Germans. You

34

spoke the language, were a good man in a tough corner. He said you were in the Royal Air Force and you had a pilot's licence.'

My head shot up at this.

'Oh, he did, did he?'

I began to see, although dimly, in what role I was being cast. 'I didn't fly in the RAF,' I said, 'that was for officers and gentlemen. I was one of the ungentlemanly officers in the RAF Regiment – one of the "roughs". My flying life has been strictly civilian.'

Kerensky nodded. Clarence had told him that.

'But tell me this,' I said, 'how did you become aware that somebody was on to your guilty secret?'

Kerensky explained that the first hint of trouble was the disappearance of the Kerensky file from Clarence's Hill Street office several weeks ago. Clarence had reported the disappearance to him with great dismay since the file was held permanently in a safe of confidential files to which normally he alone had access. When he began a rigorous check of his staff and those of his partners, one of his junior articled clerks left without giving a day's notice. Enquiries at his home revealed that he had disappeared from the island. He had left a note saying he was fed up with life in Jersey and had gone to London. He had been registered as missing but no trace of him had been found in London or anywhere else.

Yesterday the real danger signals had appeared. Clarence had received a telephone call from a man who spoke with a German accent.

'He said he knew the meeting of the Kerensky Trust was scheduled for Monday and that the plane was taking off from Jersey,' Kerensky said, raising weary eyes towards me. 'He made a vague threat saying he hoped that the Trust members would behave sensibly to avoid violence. He added only that there would be more detailed instructions later and hung up.'

Kerensky had difficulty with his breathing as he recalled the trauma of this news. 'It was after receiving this call that he decided to cable you and ask you to come to Jersey.'

I said nothing. Still I didn't understand why Clarence had been killed. I had another pull at my drink, lit another cigarette from the inlaid box. I opened my mouth to say something but Kerensky got in first.

'Then last night just before your arrival I had a telephone call from my brother Joseph who had already left Avignon to travel to Jersey for the meeting. He has changed his name to Croissé, because he has lived in France for some years. He is now Joseph Croissé. He phoned from Lyon in a near-hysterical state. Before he left Avignon his house was invaded by three armed men.'

He paused again because of his breathing difficulties. When he continued his voice was barely audible.

'His wife and daughter are being held hostage in their own house by the three men.'

It sank into my head very slowly.

'They are held against his return to make sure he and you and your other brother behave in a certain way at the meeting,' I said. He nodded. 'And no doubt they spoke French with German accents?'

Kerensky nodded again. His face was drained of colour.

But he was clearly relieved that he had told somebody else of his burden. He looked at me expectantly, as if he thought I might be able to do something immediately about the ugly situation.

'Why did you assume the German voice on the phone to Clarence was *East* German?' I asked suddenly. 'Did he say he was? Did you not imagine he might be a common-or-garden West German crook of some kind? Or even somebody assuming a German accent?'

Kerensky looked mystified. 'Clarence talked immediately of East Germans,' he said. 'It never occurred to me to query . . .' He left the sentence unfinished.

I said nothing. I was puzzled by that. Why had Clarence assumed the German voice was a Communist one? Had he known more than he'd told Kerensky?

'I managed to get Clarence by telephone just before he left for the airport to meet you,' Kerensky continued. 'I arranged to meet him at his office to tell him of the Avignon development.' He gave me another haggard, pathetic glance. 'That, I am sorry to say, is why Clarence missed having dinner with you.'

'That was only the beginning of a lot of things Clarence is going to miss now,' I said.

Rodica Kerensky glared at me. The unnatural brightness of her eyes betrayed that she was biting back angry words in her father's defence. Unaccountably at that moment I remembered the noises made by the taxi-driver. He'd been right.

'You still don't seem very well disposed towards us, Mr Robson,' she said, managing to keep her voice even. The effort caused a tremulous heaving of her breasts under the loose gown. 'Even so I think perhaps we have the right now to ask you whether you are prepared to help my father, or not.'

Her wide mouth was composed and full, not pursed as the words might have left it. Her eyes were round and steady on me, her chin lifted slightly. Kerensky was silent and hunched in his chair and didn't move when the telephone rang in the hall.

Neither did she. Then it stopped ringing. I heard the voice of a woman with a Portuguese accent answering it. I still hadn't told them my decision – mainly because I still didn't know it myself – when the maid came into the room.

'Excuse me, sir,' she said to Kerensky from behind my back, 'ees thees jentleman Meester Robson?'

He nodded.

'There ees a call for 'im, sir . . . from a Meester Hartmann.'

I got up to go to the phone.

'That was the face in the tunnel,' I said.

Nine

I was back in the room within thirty seconds. Neither Kerensky nor his daughter had moved. Their two faces, turned towards me, looked as if they were held taut by a single wire. They wouldn't have made much of the conversation from listening to my end of it. All I'd said was 'Yes' at the beginning and 'Yes' at the end.

'Where is Les Landes?' I asked. 'I believe there are some old German bunkers there.'

'Not a mile from here,' said Kerensky.

'I'll need a car. I'm going there now.'

37

'Is that wise, is it safe?' Rodica Kerensky asked quickly, glancing anxiously from me to her father and back.

'I don't know. Hartmann simply said he wanted to talk with me. I doubt if they would want to spread dead bodies all over Jersey at this stage.'

'Please be careful,' she said. But I doubted whether she was worried about my safety. I was their last chance. 'You can take my Spitfire,' she added.

'Does this mean you have agreed to help us, Mr Robson?' Kerensky put in.

'No, it doesn't mean that at all,' I replied. 'By talking to Hartmann and his thugs I might at least find out what they plan to do. I have some idea of how these men work. I don't think it's a trap for me, although I can't be sure.'

I heard myself saying this – and wondered why I *was* getting involved.

'But at last I shall have a clearer picture of what you're up against by talking to them,' I said. 'And what I'd be up against if I try to help you.' I walked out into the hall. 'And I'd better go now before I have time to think better of getting in even this deep.'

Rodica Kerensky followed me out, gave me the keys to her car and directions.

'Would you like to take the dogs?'

I smiled at her naïvety. 'I shall need more than dogs against these men if they start to cut up rough. And if they don't I expect I should fall over the dogs' leads and they'd finish up savaging *me*.'

The white Triumph Spitfire was the latest Mark Four. Its small engine announced itself immediately with a healthy tenor note when I turned the key and splashed the accelerator. Weeks held the gates open and I spurted into the lane. In my mirror I saw him shaking his head at the ugly abrasions in his neatly raked gravel. I'd let the clutch up too quickly.

The moon was high and bright now. It lit the road ahead and the empty fields with a milky-white light. I quickly reached the road skirting Les Landes and turned into the first rutted track that ran off to the right through high bushes of spiky gorse.

Les Landes turned out to be a desolate, barren expanse of open land reaching to the cliff edges of the island's north–west corner. The hulks of German bunkers rising out of every hollow along the pitted tracks gave the place an a'r of threat and menace. Fire had recently swept the gorse and now only twisted, black, skeletal hands thrust themselves up from the ash-covered surface.

I drove slowly past giant concrete saucers sunk into the cliff-top by Hitler's men. They still retained the rusting tooth-wheel mechanisms that had once swung long-barrelled guns to command the surrounding sea.

The petrol in the tank behind my ears swooshed and slopped noisily as the Triumph rose and sank sharply in the deep ruts of the track. In the moonlit darkness the scarred landscape looked hopeless and sour like the surface of a dead planet. God seemed to have forsaken Les Landes shortly after the Germans did in 1945. I regretted leaving the safe, civilized drawing-room in the fortified farmhouse.

A flock of small birds rose suddenly from the ground under the offside wing, startling me. They scattered through the groping yellow fingers of the headlights. I peered ahead through the windscreen looking for the concrete tower that Hartmann had directed me to.

The sound of the sea was a continuous roar from the foot of the cliff now. This meant I was nearing the edge.

I rose erratically over a hump, swinging the wheel from side to side to avoid the axle-breaking holes and came in sight of the tower.

It stood blackly solid against the light the moon spilled on the sea. It was crenellated down one side. The three cut-away balconies protected narrow observation slits that ran round the half circle of the seaward side of the tower. From its flat top jutted the rusted iron mounting of a swivel gun, long dismantled. I bumped to a standstill fifty yards short of the tower, turned the car round to point in the direction I'd come, switched off the lights and got out.

I stood for a moment clutching the black, rubber Ever Ready torch Rodica Kerensky had given me. It was not just my only way of seeing, it was my only weapon. When I moved, the ground had a hollow ring beneath my feet. I guessed I was standing on underground quarters and ammunition chambers built in support of the self-contained gun emplacements.

There was no sign of a light, no cars to indicate the presence of the East Germans. Perhaps they hadn't arrived yet. They must have used a telephone box – unless they'd found an old field telephone left in the bunkers by their Nazi forbears to call Kerensky's house.

The wind moaned through the stunted gorse and the sea wrestled noisily with the rocks eighty feet below. The moon suddenly stopped scattering its light on the sea as a thick cloud snuffed it out.

I decided I must either get back in the car now and scuttle off the moor or go into the bunker.

I slithered down into an eight-foot gully that led to the base of the tower. Twenty yards short of it the left bank suddenly turned to concrete and a series of doorways led into the cement catacombs. I stopped and ran the spot beam of the torch up the wall. It showed me a fresco of a pair of Nazi jackboots painted beside the doorway. The paint was fresh looking, black with yellow and white highlights. Above the door itself in the same colours was the one enigmatic word 'IT'.

Unless Hartmann had suddenly developed a flippant sense of humour he hadn't had in Berlin, I guessed this was the work of summer hippies. They had probably used the bunkers as a rent-free quarters for sleep-ins and love-ins. Above the second door in red paint that looked much older it said 'SICK BAY'.

I took a firmer grip on the torch and stepped into the bunker. I hoped this wasn't 'IT'. The thin finger of light from my torch poked aside the blackness that smelled faintly of stale tar and dust.

A loud crack split the silence. I jumped. When I touched down again I swung the beam round me fast into all corners of the oppressive vault.

'Keep Cool!'

The advice was printed in green capital letters on the red-and-white plastic Jersey Real Fruit Yoghurt cup that had splintered resoundingly under my right foot. 'Eat on day of purchase or within four days if kept in a refrigerator,' said the grinning head of a Jersey cow with a daisy in its mouth.

I tiptoed on into the massive stone corridors. My torch showed me empty, vault-like rooms similar to the first one. I don't know why I tiptoed after announcing my entrance with the empty yoghurt cup. But I did.

'Parazone Exterminates Germs,' a discarded plastic bottle told me. I kicked something soggy wrapped in newspaper and hurried on. I was ducking constantly to avoid rusting water and air-dust pipes jutting out of the walls.

In another vault I stopped and sniffed again but the air was arid, featureless. I returned to the entrance and gave up expecting anything from this bunker.

Then in the doorway I saw something. I bent and picked up two slips of paper charred at the edges. They were numbered fifty and fifty-one. I peered closer with my torch. In pencil on blue-lined receipt-book paper it said, '24/11/69 La Collette Promenade. To transport of men and haulage of rubble: 9 hours'.

I dropped them back on the floor, walked out into the dark air of the gully and turned left towards the tower.

Ten

As my feet crunched on the gravel in the bottom of the gully I shaded the torch over my wrist and looked at my watch. One fourteen. I'd spent nearly ten minutes in the first bunker. Still no sign of cars or lights.

I looked up at the broad turret above me and wondered if Hartmann was watching my approach. If Rodica Kerensky had asked me now if I thought it was safe to come, if I thought there was no possibility of a trap, I would not have answered so confidently. A body tucked away in the deserted Nazi crypts and covered with rubble might remain undiscovered for years.

To get to the tower I had to go to the brink of the cliff. From there it was a straight plunge to where the rocks were whipping the sea into a detergent froth, mixing in moonlight for that extra whiteness.

I turned quickly into the narrow entrance and stopped to listen.

Take two identical empty buildings. Leave one empty and put a human being out of sight in the darkness in the other. Then go and stand in each one in turn and listen. You will find the same silence has different qualities.

The silence was as thick in the tower as it had been in the bunker but I sensed an indefinable presence. I painted the circular walls quickly with streaks of yellow torchlight. The ground floor chamber was empty. The six-inch fortified slit built in a semi-hexagonal shape looked out to sea – and let in a horizontal wedge of faint light. A narrow spiral staircase to my left led up to the second and third levels.

I ran up the steps two at a time with the torch pointing six inches ahead of my toe-caps.

'Klaus!'

The voice rang loudly from the top chamber.

At that moment I reached the second level and something hard was jabbed between my shoulder blades from behind.

'*Stehen bleiben, bitte!*'

The words were shouted from close to my left ear.

My reactions are quick. Speed off the mark helps to make up for inadequacies in depth. I fetched the torch up from knee level, pressing the rubber button to extinguish it at the same moment. I was bringing it over and through with my other hand joining itself on to the grip in an exaggerated golf swing before I had time to think whether it was a good idea or not. My nerves had been stretched taut for so long waiting for something that they twanged of their own accord.

The two-handed swing caught Klaus in the neck under the ear. The torch came on again under the impact of the blow and spun from my grasp. As I fell sideways to the floor with the force of the follow-through I saw Klaus staggering back against the wall. The metal object he had poked between my shoulder blades flew up, then down. And as it struck the floor three yards from my head there was a deafening roar.

The impact had detonated the trigger.

I pressed my face to the cold, dusty floor and covered it with my arms as the discharged bullet zipped and sang, ricocheting round the circular walls like an angry bluebottle buzzing against closed windows. I heard it clatter to a stop and fall spent half-way up the spiral to the next level.

A brighter light snapped on from above. It was one of those madly-efficient German lamps with a headlight in front and another on top that can flash quick, slow, at delayed intervals, red or white – in fact, do everything except wash the dishes after supper.

Hartmann's face appeared beside it looking down. He had those deep-set eyes that hide under an overhanging cliff of forehead-and-eyebrows, leaving the sockets looking like dark holes into the head. Only when he lifted his face into a direct light was the skull-like effect relieved by the sight of his eyes. With his head held beside the lamp his eyes remained invisible.

Klaus was picking himself up, rubbing a shoulder, swearing softly and looking menacing. Hartmann motioned him to get his gun and cover me. Then he addressed words in my direction.

'*Guten Abend, Herr Robson. Es gefällt mir sehr, dass wir uns noch einmal wiedersehen.*'

His expression didn't match his words of welcome.

'*Es jefällt mir jar nicht, Hartmann,*' I said, raising myself to one elbow but remaining otherwise prone. I parodied his Berlin accent, softening the g's to j's, telling him the meeting didn't please me. Hartmann was a Berlin Cockney and didn't like being reminded of it.

'What are you doing up there with that great light?' I asked, keeping to Berlin-accented German. 'Signalling to the population of Jersey that the Germans are back in command of the island?'

Hartmann didn't smile, didn't reply. Instead he walked to the top of the steps, came down the first three and stooped to pick up something. He held up what looked like a large, misshapen penny that had been placed on a railway line and mutilated by a rather fast express train.

'Lucky for you they are not, Herr Robson,' he said in German, waving the spent bullet in front of him as he came down the rest of the flight. 'Otherwise we would have to prosecute you for using a torch as a dangerous weapon.'

'And put me in a concentration camp no doubt?' I said, still aping his Berlin accent.

43

He didn't let the jibe rile him.

'Perhaps . . . if you were lucky,' he said absently. 'You may get up now,' he added, waving Klaus forward to do a quick search for a weapon.

When he didn't find one, Klaus picked up my torch, turned it off and went to stand with his back to a wall where he could keep his eye and gun on me.

I dusted myself down, placed both hands flat behind the base of my spine and leaned them and me against the cold gritty wall.

'I'm not used to being invited to discussions then being welcomed with a gun in my back, Hartmann,' I said, by way of explaining my behaviour. I nodded exaggeratedly towards Klaus and said I hoped I hadn't hurt him too much. He glowered at me and hunched his shoulders twice in a quick nervous movement.

'Shining the light from up there would not signal anything to the Jerseymen since the aperture faces only seawards,' said Hartmann. He was about three questions behind. 'And since the light was shone from below the level of the aperture, neither the residents of Guernsey nor passing seamen on their ships would be aware of our presence.'

Hartmann was demonstrating his cool superior logic, his cool superior German mind. I decided to indulge him, still using his language – but without the Berlin accent.

'Why did you ask me to come here?'

Hartmann stopped wandering around the stone chamber. The wind sliced through the slit from the sea like the horizontal blade of a guillotine. He turned and shone his lamp in my face.

'To warn you. To advise you. To suggest certain things.'

The empty cavities where his eyes should have been appeared beside the light which was making me blink. 'I should hate the same thing to happen to you as happened to your friend and our enemy – Clarence Smythe.'

'Why did you kill him, you crude Kraut!' I said viciously. I reverted to English unthinkingly in my anger.

Klaus shifted off the wall and moved towards me, looking expectantly towards Hartmann. He waved Klaus back and considered me with a slightly wagging head. Eventually he turned away and spoke to the open sea through the slit.

'It wasn't part of our plan. Let's say Smythe thought he was too clever, thought he could outmanoeuvre us because he once had the protection of his uniform in Berlin.' He stood looking out to sea for several moments with the lamp pointing at the floor behind his back. 'Perhaps it will act as a warning to all concerned not to do other than those things which we might direct.'

Hartmann seemed to think that by constructing tortured sentences in his native tongue he might nullify his Berlin accent which he had never managed to erase.

I did a bit more cursing on Clarence's behalf, using short English words: But they both remained unmoved this time.

'You should advise your principals,' Hartmann said after a while, still without turning round, 'to comply with our instructions. Otherwise . . .' He allowed the sentence to hang unfinished.

'Otherwise there will be an accident in Avignon?' I suggested helpfully.

I could see him nodding in silhouette against the slit of moonlit sea. But I didn't catch his '*Ja*' if, in fact, he uttered it.

'So you have heard? Good,' he said at last.

'Don't talk of the Kerenskys as *my* principals,' I said. 'I'm not on anybody's side. I'm just an accidental observer.'

'*Wirklich? Wirklich?*' Hartmann expressed mock surprise. 'You mean poor Captain Smythe died before he could tell you of his plans to foil us with your help?' He had lit a thin cheroot that smelled so badly it could only have come from Bulgaria. 'Then you would be well advised to remain neutral.'

'Unless of course you offer me a twenty-fifth share to help *you*,' I put in casually. 'Hadn't you thought to buy me for a million?'

'I think we can manage by ourselves, *danke schön*,' Hartmann said softly, rocking back and forward on his heels and bending forward to peer through the slit more intently.

I shifted my hands off the wall and straightened up. I was getting cramped. I chafed my hands together in front of me, doing it carefully under the close gaze of Klaus. He had a face over which the skin was stretched tight. A long straight nose and close-set narrow eyes made it a face that warned without needing to resort to expression.

A bat flew in the door of the tower and began banging blindly against the circular inner wall below. It rose up into the chamber where we stood in its blind panic, diving and swooping, making shrill, squeaking cries. Hartmann suddenly ducked and moved wildly, trying to avoid it. I raised an arm to keep the bat out of my face as it threshed the air towards me. Klaus stood immobile. Only his eyes moved, following the bat's erratic flight. The gun in his right hand never wavered from its line on me.

Hartmann thrashed his arms around above his head. The bat, as if responding to his panic, fluttered and knocked against the wall around him.

'Get that damned thing out of here,' he said to Klaus.

But Klaus, instead of loosing off a volley of shots at it, sensibly stood impassive. The bat ran full tilt into the wall and flopped and slithered down the stairs to the ground chamber. After a moment it rose, got its echo-sounding equipment working again, found the doorway and was gone.

The tower was silent once more. Hartmann turned his back again and stood quiet.

His posture of impenetrable calm strength had been dented. I turned my head to stare at Klaus. I thought I saw a spark of vicarious embarrassment there for the behaviour of his superior.

So Hartmann, I thought, you don't always live up to your translated name 'Hard Man'.

'At least they haven't managed to blow up your bunkers here, Hartmann,' I said, trying to get a little salt in the pinprick. 'There's always that.'

He still wasn't looking at me or Klaus.

'You know why your countrymen built such good fortifications in Jersey, Hartmann?' I went on. 'They wanted to avoid getting sent to the Russian front – snow, frostbite, mud, and sudden death. They rather wanted to stay in sunny Jersey, sunbathing on the beach in their off-duty hours and flirting with any local girls that would. So they put heart and soul into these bunkers and the sea-wall along St Ouen's Bay. Some of the best fortifications ever built. Pity they were never used of course – but then we never had any intention of invading the islands, you know. We, too, wanted a few divisions of German troops to stay here idling around.'

Suddenly he turned on me. His Berlin accent coarsened as his temper rose. 'You know better than most, Robson,' he shouted, 'that we and the people in the Party in the German Democratic Republic were either in prison, in concentration camps or sheltering in the Soviet Union when the fascist Hitlerites were bringing shame on Germany.' He didn't try to conceal his anger. I was pleased. 'The anti-fascist struggle is continuing in the DDR today. It has been waged for many years by those who want to build Socialism and lead the German people on the road to Communism,' he mouthed fiercely.

'What about those people in the Party and government who can be found in the old Nazi-party lists? Perhaps not as many as in West Germany but they're there, just the same,' I said without any enthusiasm for the tattered topic, but just to keep his back up.

He lowered his voice, regaining control. 'There were people who were drawn into the Nazi party by pressure. Those in our party have had a genuine change of heart. And they were all minor members. Not like the revanchist Nazis who still hold high places in Bonn.'

He flicked the light back and forth in my face to aggravate me, forgetting that my head was level with the seaward slit. But I didn't trouble to remind him.

'So now what do you want with twenty-five million pounds of dirty capitalist money?' I asked.

'Safeguarding Socialism costs money . . .' he began.

'You mean like invading Czechoslovakia, for instance? Planning to invade someone else in the Warsaw Pact, are you? Romania? Or even non-aligned Yugoslavia?'

Hartmann's eyes suddenly appeared from the shadows of their sockets. They bulged. 'Lenin laid down that any means was justified by the end. If we use capitalist money to overthrow capitalism, we are following a Leninist principle.'

'But what exactly do you want the twenty-five million capital for?' I persisted, still trying to needle him.

He had calmed down enough to let out an unpleasant bark of laughter.

'Do you think the Warsaw Pact countries have taken to announcing the intentions of their security agencies to Western news hacks, Robson?' He leered at his own humour. 'When we do, I promise you, you will be the first to be informed. But rest assured that we are at present mounting a costly project for which we need a considerable amount of Western currency.'

'I think I'll refer to it as 'The German Stratagem' from now on,' I said airily. 'It's a very appropriate title for your operation. Do you know why?'

Hartmann was lighting another foul-smelling cheroot and didn't answer.

'If you spell "stratagem" backwards, it becomes "Mega-Tarts." Another way of saying "Big Ladies of Easy Virtue". So it's a very apt codename for your group from East Berlin, isn't it?'

All trace of humour suddenly evaporated from Hartmann's face and he scowled; such was the sourness of the expression I immediately decided to change tack. Needling, I could see, might easily become counterproductive.

'Okay, if you won't venture an opinion on Operation German Stratagem,' I said, adopting a more confidential, admiring tone, 'Tell me how you got on to the Kerenskys.'

'Robson,' Hartmann was speaking wearily, 'I didn't ask you here to dictate my memoirs or the innermost secrets of the Kremlin. I invited you here to warn you. We know you were a freelance journalist in Berlin. But we are not so foolish as to discount the possibility that you might also conceivably work for other organizations in London.'

'We don't use journalists as spies,' I said slowly, 'unlike Communist countries.'

'Really,' said Hartmann raising the eyebrows above the black holes in his face. 'Then what about your Mr Philby? I thought he was some kind of journalist. I don't think you can claim it's unknown, Herr Robson.'

I said nothing. I concentrated on looking outraged at the idea of journalist spies.

'But I will give you a kind of answer to your question,' he went on. 'Or rather I will direct your attention to a certain irony. Not for publication of course. I hope you will regard the whole of our talk as "off the record".' He laughed the grating bark of laughter again at his own urbanity.

'I imagine we are right in thinking you came to Jersey as a personal favour to your friend Symthe and that you are respecting confidences. You are not a newspaperman first, in this island.' Hartmann went on without waiting for a reply. 'The irony you might not have appreciated without my guidance is this. The tax havens of your Western world are the inner sanctums of private capital. In them the sated symbols of your doomed way of life, the overfed, over-indulged millionaires cluster like bees round a honey pot, protecting their massive personal fortunes in a last stand against grasping capitalist governments.'

He paused to squash the evil-smelling Bulgarian cheroot beneath his heel.

'What better hunting grounds could be found for the representatives of the People's Democracies? The tax havens are the soft, unguarded underbellies of the capitalist world. Small, independent islands or states, without large security organs at their disposal. A lot of money coming and going in shady deals, depending mainly on secrecy. Is the irony beginning to dawn on you, Herr Robson?'

I admitted it was beginning to dawn on me.

'What's happened to the boy from Clarence Smythe's office, who disappeared with the file?' I said suddenly. But he didn't reply. Or change his expression.

Instead he said, 'It is perfect, isn't it? Find a quasi-illegal organization that under no circumstances can afford to appeal to the protection of law, disposing of a large sum of money. Then take your fruit basket and hold it under the ripe plum until it falls.'

'I love your old German proverbs,' I said, sniffing and rubbing my cold hands together. 'Can we go soon please, Hartmann, before another bat flies in?'

He stiffened for a moment then relaxed again. 'Tell Kerensky we have all the papers prepared for him and his brothers to sign on Monday. We shall contact you then about how we shall go about it. Just tell them to co-operate sensibly.'

He turned back to peer out of the slit again. 'Oh, and Herr Robson, go back to London and keep quiet,' he said over his shoulder. 'Unless you want an accident in Avignon – or even in Jersey. Of course, we prefer to avoid accidents where we can. That's why I asked you here.'

I shifted from one foot to the other, cold creeping up my legs. The draught from the slit was still trying to chop through my clothes.

'I wonder if I might go now, please,' I said respectfully.

'All right, Klaus,' he said, still without turning round.

Klaus pushed me in front of him towards the staircase with the butt of the pistol – hard enough to make a largish bruise in the area of my kidneys within a few hours: I grunted and went quickly down the steps. Klaus stayed in the doorway.

I turned back suddenly and reached towards him. 'I wonder if I might have the torch back – it isn't mine you see.'

Klaus hesitated. Then Hartmann called out from above for him to give me it.

I took the Ever Ready from his reluctant grip. '*Auf Wiedersehen*,' I called into the darkness of the tower. There was no reply. I walked quickly up the gully and got into the car. Shivering slightly, I started the engine, turned on the heater and drove as fast as I dared towards the road. I thought of waiting to see where their unseen car would head for. But I'd had enough for one night.

The heater had just begun to warm me when I pulled up outside the white gates of the Kerensky farmhouse. Inside, he and his daughter still sat in the same chairs in the drawing-room with the same anxious expressions on their faces as when I left.

I gave them a brief account of what happened, drank another large whisky to chase the last vestiges of cold away and suggested that bed was the best place for me – and for them too.

As I closed the drawing-room door I heard Rodica Kerensky go over to her father's chair and make consoling noises.

Eleven

I was glad to be alone and fling off my clothes in the bedroom. Or rather the dressing-room connected to the bedroom through an open arch. There was also a bathroom *en suite*, as a house agent would have said.

I smelled sour — not only from the running in the town. The sweating in the bunker had not been from exertion.

I went to play with the gleaming chrome equipment on the bath, wash basin, shower and bidet. Jets hissed and steamed. I pulled levers and twisted taps, raised and lowered automatic stoppers. There was a tap that worked like a joy-stick of an aeroplane, giving hot water in the up position, cold in the down and greater and lesser pressure when pulled side-to-side. I worked away at this busily for a time but the house seemed to stay on the ground as far as I could see.

I wandered around towelling myself in a thermostatically-controlled state of nudity.

The bedroom and dressing-room were decorated in pale pastel shades. There was heavy, damask curtaining. Fleecy rugs were scattered around the thickly carpeted floor. Wardrobes with white louvred doors lined one wall, as they do in those luxurious pictures in the Sunday colour supplements. Kerensky had said how he admired his daughter's taste and left the interior of the house entirely to her judgement.

I stopped to scrutinize a frame of signed Annigoni pencil drawings of male nude figures as I climbed into my pyjama trousers.

I lay down on the bed without bothering to put on my pyjama jacket. Perhaps it was Annigoni's influence. I switched out the light and hoped the tension of the night would ease away in the warm cradle the central heating was providing. I thought I would mull over the evening in detail and try to decide whether I wanted a hundred and fifty thousand pounds enough to risk ending my untidy existence on or before Monday.

'Born 19 July 1936. Died 3 October 1972.'

They wouldn't put up a plinth for me like Pierre Le Sueur — but at least I'd have that neat start and finish.

I only realized that I had fallen asleep when I woke. I'd drawn back the curtain on a window facing into the fortified courtyard before getting into the bed. The faint light of the moon, now sailing well down the sky, still shone thinly into the room. But it was enough for me to see that the room had changed since I'd turned out the light.

I wasn't alone any longer.

Perhaps it was my nose not my eyes that told me first. Then I saw the figure was moving across the room towards the bed. I realized that it had been the click of the door closing that had finally dragged me back to consciousness. And unless the East Germans had taken to wearing expensive French perfume, I thought I was fairly certain who my visitor was.

She stood for a moment by the bed. I hadn't moved and she seemed uncertain whether my eyes were open, whether I was asleep or awake. By the light from the window behind her I could see she wore nightclothes, a heavier, loose robe over something long and flimsy.

I wondered for a moment if I was dreaming myself into some kind of hackneyed melodrama. Was she the villainess who would take a stiletto from the loose, dark folds and plunge it to the hilt in my bare breast?

I felt the side of the bed give gently under her weight. That was real enough. Brushing the hair back from her face with one hand she looked down at me. I watched through almost-closed eyes. The perfume was stronger now and I could smell, too, the clean, brown warmth of her body as she leaned over me.

Her mouth was warm and moist when it reached me and as her lips parted I felt her teeth taking a gentle grip on a tiny pucker of flesh an inch above the waistband of my pyjamas. She shook her head in a little sideways motion, worrying the pucker of flesh playfully like a puppy. The heavy fall of her breasts brushed my chest. As she moved her head, her hair swung down to cover her face.

I reached out my hands and raked them through the hair until they reached her ears. I tugged them lightly until I freed her teeth from their hold and pulled her round to face me, raising my head from the pillow.

She breathed unevenly through parted lips but her expression was hidden by the rich tumble of hair. The front of the robe was open and the full weight of her breasts rested on me through the thin nightdress.

I reached sideways and snapped on the bedside light.

'You're not really very good at this,' I said roughly. 'Did your father send you?'

Rodica Kerensky sat back startled in the sudden glare of the light. She was breathing fast – from anger now. She pulled her blue woollen robe quickly round in front of her and held it high at the neck, her eyes wide, her nostrils flaring.

'Do you think I'm some kind of bullet-headed thug, who can be bought with a bit of cheap seduction?' I shot at her.

'You behave like a bullet-headed thug!' she snapped back. She moved backwards along the bed and stood up, her arms folded tightly in front of her, glaring. 'And my father didn't send me; get that out of your head! It's probably impossible for anybody as insensitive as you to understand an unselfish act.'

'There's no such thing as an unselfish act,' I said. 'A lot of people help others to make themselves feel better.'

She tossed her head and the copper hair swung back over her shoulders. 'I would do anything for my father!' She spat out the words. 'Anything! The years in Auschwitz took a great toll on him. My mother didn't survive those years. He has worked hard for what he has won. And given unselfishly to me. He needs help now more than ever before. Do you think I'm going to stand by and see him blackmailed, kidnapped or killed, without doing everything I can to help?'

She paused for breath, her breasts and folded arms rising and falling fast. 'Even if it means . . . if it means resorting to this.' She pulled a face that conveyed self-disgust.

'Why don't you sit down,' I said quietly.

After a moment she sat at the foot of the bed, putting as much distance between us as possible. I got up and put on a dressing-gown, offered her one of my cigarettes, lit them and stood looking down at her.

'Perhaps I haven't behaved as well as I might towards you and your father,' I said with a shrug. 'But Clarence Smythe was my friend not my lawyer.' I drew hard on my cigarette. 'And perhaps you might like to look at things from where I'm standing. People I've never met before who are running a devious, multi-million international swindle ask me to try to protect them single-handed from some very nasty professional spies. Men who clearly don't think twice about killing those who stand between them and what they want.'

'Don't you at least want revenge for Clarence's death?'

'Revenge.' I laughed. 'It wouldn't bring him back to life would it? And I might not survive the attempt.'

'Are you a coward then?' She flung the words down challengingly.

'Probably. But at least I don't behave like a character in a novelette, reacting to clumsy attempts at seduction and insults to my courage and sense of heroism.'

She bent her head suddenly.

'I'm sorry,' she said, quietly hugging herself, still on the edge of the bed. The apology was a visible effort. Millionaires' daughters don't spend a lot of their time apologizing. 'I'm not behaving very sensibly. My father and I have been living on our nerves.'

We smoked in silence for a while.

Then she looked at me again, a trace of anger edging back into her expression. 'But stop being so damned condescending and using words like "swindle" and "fiddle". There is nothing illegal about the family Trust.'

'Isn't there?' I asked.

'No, there isn't. International lawyers, accountants and bankers in every country spend a lot of time looking for loopholes in the law. And make a lot of money doing it. If you had money your attitude would change too.'

'So would my bank manager's,' I said. 'He won't speak to me at present.'

She got up and began to pace up and down. 'My father and both my uncles pay taxes on their own personal individual assets and financial dealings here and in France and Switzerland. They draw on the Trust in various ways but we're not leeches. This little island benefits well enough from the presence of people like us.'

'I suppose it's a matter of "business ethics",' I said. 'A Jewish friend of mine once gave me an illustration of what this meant to him. He said a lady came into his shop and bought an article for five pounds. Then as she walked out he discovered she'd given him two fivers stuck together. This, he said, was where business ethics had to come in.' I hunched my shoulders, spread my palms and did a Jewish merchant's voice. 'The question of ethics was this – "Should I tell my partner, or should I not tell my partner?"'

The look Rodica Kerensky gave me would have served equally well for somebody who had just been convicted of interfering with little boys behind wooden buildings. She bent to stub out her cigarette in an ashtray. 'If my father and his brothers can find a way to protect the source of our wealth, won at a very high price in the past, is there anybody to say they have no right to do so?'

It wasn't a question that required an answer. I sat down on the bed myself to avoid her agitated pacing. She clenched her elbows tight in front of her.

'People like us suffered enough in Europe under Hitler to last a thousand years. Who are you to stand in moral judgement?'

She stood staring down at me.

'I wonder if you have any conception,' she said. 'My grandfather was born in Russia. He fled from the pogroms there and settled in Romania where my father was born. I was born there too, in 1941. Before the war my father helped build up the Romanian oil industry and was involved in opening up the gold and silver mines there, too. Romania is one of the richest countries in Europe in natural resources, but it needed money and business skill to exploit them.'

She paused, a frown creasing her face. 'But then the ugly hatred came to the boil there too. There was no gratitude. Many Jews were simply flung into the ravines of the Carpathian mountains. My father sent me to Switzerland with my uncle and aunt while he and mother moved on into Hungary. It was a mistake that was fatal for my mother.'

She began pacing again.

'The persecution was worse in Hungary. They were rounded up into a transport for Auschwitz. My mother did not survive. She walked up and down in silence for a while. 'My father did survive. But at great cost to his health. And to survive he was forced to do many things of which he was not proud.'

The frown settled deeper into her face with the pain of the memory as the words poured out. 'We were reunited in England, where my grandfather had had the sense to live. Before he died the family fortune, that had been preserved in Swiss banks, was put into the Trust.'

She stopped and looked down at me again. Her voice was lower, more controlled in its bitterness. 'Do you think the faceless, highly moral governments of Europe have some right to that money? Or have people like my father the right to do all they can to protect and preserve their own?'

I accepted the rhetorical question in silence.

She had stopped and I motioned her to sit down again. I gave her another cigarette. When she had calmed down I suggested gently that she should go back to her room. I got myself a drink and settled down, with the light on this time, to think some more.

Twelve

I woke about six thirty wondering why a bright light was shining in my eyes. Then I realized. I rolled over, reached out and switched off the bedside lamp that had been burning all night. I let myself sink back to the surface of unconsciousness – and prepared to submerge again.

Then I remembered why I'd left the light on in the first place. To think. Then I remembered what I'd thought. Then I remembered where I was. Then I rolled back, jabbed my finger at the switch again and sat up blinking.

Five minutes later I was walking quietly down the wide, carpeted corridor. It was as much a picture gallery as a corridor. But my eyes were not open wide enough to appreciate the efforts of the Old Masters who had spent time, energy and oil decorating the gilt-framed canvases on the walls.

I had reached what I guessed was Rodica Kerensky's room and was stretching out a stealthy, clenched fist when I heard a step behind me.

I turned my head quickly to find Miss Kerensky covering me with a tea-tray – the spout of the silver teapot pointing unwaveringly at my chest.

I let my knuckles, bunched to knock quietly on her door, fall to my side. Her expression was part quizzical, part contemptuous.

'You missed the first and last opportunity last night, Mr Robson, remember?'

'I was really looking for somebody to ask the time of the next train to Avignon,' I said, eyeing the tea-tray which she held steadily in front of her. 'But if that's loaded,' I said, nodding towards the teapot, 'I'd be glad of a cup of tea.'

She led the way back down to the kitchen.

I sat down at the kitchen table while she got another cup from among the several acres of china plate displayed on Welsh dressers of scrubbed pine. She poured two cups of tea without looking at me.

She wore the same long blue robe over her nightdress and turned away from me to gaze through a window into the courtyard as she sipped her tea.

'Does the joke about trains to Avignon mean you are actually condescending to help us?' she asked without looking round.

'Well, I'm not just going down to see the *pont*,' I replied through the steam from the tea.

'In that case I'll go and tell my father.'

She put down her cup and almost ran into the hall and up the stairs.

I switched on the kitchen radio and poured another cup of tea. I rubbed my chin and was wondering whether to run upstairs, too, to shave when the voice of the BBC announcer reading the seven o'clock news advised me otherwise.

'. . . the Jersey police are anxious to trace a freelance journalist, Jonathan Robson, aged 36, who they believe may be able to help them with their enquiries. A taxi-driver in St Helier told police that the murdered lawyer was with the journalist last night a few hours before he was found dead. Enquiries at the journalist's hotel revealed he had been missing since late last night . . .'

I stared at the radio for a moment. What sort of journalist was it who completely overlooked the obvious news interest in the mysterious murder of a lawyer in a holiday island? Perhaps I was losing my touch. And what sort of journalist omitted to realize how suspicious his role in the murder of his friend looked to the police? My sort, obviously.

I realized then that Rodica Kerensky had returned from upstairs and was rooted in the doorway, listening to the news bulletin.

'What will you do?' she said at last, moving from the doorway and switching off the details of the latest Common Market negotiations in Brussels.

'Go and hide out in Avignon, I suppose. Do you know a safe house there? Perhaps one with an armed guard or two?'

She stood by the table looking at me thoughtfully.

'I was going to shave,' I said apologetically, 'but that BBC fellow has made me change my mind. This seven o'clock shadow might help. Bullet-headed *and* blue-chinned. Do you think a beard would suit me?'

'You sound like the young Karl Marx now. As the great hater of accumulation of private capital you should go far with a beard,' she said drily.

I grinned at this first flash of humour. It suited her better than the tense, taut strain that I had seen on her face most of the time.

'I don't hate the accumulation of private capital *per se*,' I said. 'I just resent it being accumulated by people other than myself – and I've never been able to keep any of it long enough to accumulate.'

'That doesn't surprise me about you leftists,' she said.

'Leftists? Am I a leftist?' My expression was wounded.

'Engels left all his property in London to the relatives of Marx after he died,' she said. 'You're fine in theory but hypocritical in practice.'

'That makes me feel much better then,' I said, 'that's normal at least.'

She smiled as she turned away to stack the teacups at the sink for the Portuguese staff.

'I only want to go as far as Avignon, with or without the beard,' I mused. 'That involves crossing about thirty-five miles of Channel to the French coast then about another six hundred miles to the south . . . I suppose you have to show your passport to go over to France?'

58

She nodded. 'Unless you go for a day trip on the hydrofoil to St Malo. Then the shipping company issues you with a sort of pink identity card with your photograph on it.'

'Really? That's interesting.' I began to plan. 'Can your father organize a quick car to be waiting at St Malo?' I asked.

'I should think so; he has friends in Brittany.'

'Good. Ask him to arrange it will you.'

'What are you going to do when you reach Avignon? Is three to one very good odds?'

'Not very good at all. All I will have is a short start in surprising them. I haven't really thought how I shall go about it. I shall sort of rely on instantaneous, Errol Flynn-style inspiration on the spot. Dive bullet-headed through French windows brandishing cutlass, swing across room on chandelier catching two of them in throat with high heels of sea boots. That sort of thing. But if all else fails I'll revert to my basic policy.'

'And what's that?' she asked dubiously.

'When in doubt, run in circles, scream and shout.'

She was already half-way upstairs to her father's room when she stopped and turned, one hand on the banister. 'The hydrofoil leaves every morning at nine fifteen so you haven't much time. Weeks has some old clothes that might tone in with your beard.'

Then she swept on again, holding the long robe clear of the ground with her left hand. It cost a lot of money at finishing schools in Switzerland to learn to walk upstairs like that.

At a minute past nine I walked into Woolworths in King Street, St Helier. At least I think it was me. I caught sight of a reflection in one of those mirrors on the pillars between the counters. It showed a scruffy, down-at-heel hippy in a maroon tee-shirt, and a pair of faded jeans that might have once been grey under Weeks's mud stains. The apparition wore a pair of spectacles with gold wire frames and his hair was combed forward over his forehead and ears in a style that would have won the approval of Titus Andronicus.

I scratched my nose with my right hand and the reflection did the same, so I suppose that confirmed it was me.

I pulled back the short green curtains of a 'Photograph Yourself' booth and sat down inside. I stared inanely at my reflection in the little black window as the light flashed five times. For the third picture I took the glasses off and half-closed my eyes to make them look drawn and shivelled as they do on people who wear spectacles.

I leaned against the outside of the booth and picked my nose while waiting to see what developed. Perhaps I was overdoing the role, I thought, when two young dolly shop assistants nudged each other then turned away in disgust. So I just leaned and looked permissive.

I took the little strip of five pictures back to the Triumph. Rodica Kerensky shuddered when she looked at them. Then she drove me to the Commodore Shipping office in Conway Street.

The girl behind the counter there preferred one with the glasses on. She didn't exactly hold it at arm's length between finger and thumb. But she was doing it mentally as I gave her a squinting look through a pair of Kerensky's glasses – which made things look blurred beyond six feet from my nose.

But my vision wasn't too blurred to see my reflection in the front of the *Daily Express* a man was reading beside me. A photograph of how I had looked yesterday stared out of the front page. The headline said: 'Press Man Sought in Island Murder Riddle.' The cleverly-worded story said I was 'missing' and there were 'fears for my safety' to get round the legal niceties of printing my picture.

I turned and peered intently into the street at nothing. I pulled a hand over my hair from crown to forehead, flattening it down towards my eyebrows. I wished I could cover my whole face.

It would have been hard for any mother to be proud of the face leering out of the Woolworths photograph. But I decided to decrease the chances of recognition by keeping my head down and mumbling answers to the girl selling the tickets.

If I got involved with the police now there would be no trip to Avignon.

At that precise moment I decided I was Frank Smith, commercial artist, aged 28 – unforgivable vanity I suppose – of 20 Ovington Gardens, Knightsbridge, born at Loughborough.

The girl stapled Frank's photograph on to a pink identity card issued by the States of Jersey Customs and Excise and asked me to fill in my name, address and date and place of birth in three different places. The French would tear bits off it when I landed and left and the Jersey immigration authorities would like to keep the photograph for their files on my return, she said. The card would be valid for sixty hours.

At the Albert Pier I dragged an old rucksack from the back of the Triumph. It contained my suit, shirt, tie, toothbrush and the black, rubber Ever Ready torch. I leaned towards the window of the Triumph, speaking loudly. 'Thanks, Lupin, for the ride. Go back to your flowerbed now, while Louis the Leftist bombs down to the St Malo scene.'

I leered permissively and shambled towards the customs shed and the Condor 1 Hydrofoil drawn up at the dockside with its spidery feet sunk in the still water.

The Triumph did not pull away immediately. I suspected Rodica Kerensky was waiting to wave me Good Luck. I resisted the urge to indulge in any display of bourgeois sentimentality and kept on without looking round, past the uniformed police cat who was scrutinizing the faces of passengers. The immigration officer didn't trouble to conceal his distaste at my appearance. But Frank Smith caused him and the other uniformed fuzz standing at his side no more than momentary annoyance. I gave them a look that indicated I didn't dig their scene and hunched across the gangplank on to the Condor.

Thirteen

After moving sluggishly through the smooth water of the harbour the hydrofoil got up off its knees and planed swiftly over the thirty-five miles to St Malo. It swooped over the waves of the Channel flinging spray back against its cabin windows. I bought a bottle of Hine Cognac duty free and stuffed it in my rucksack. I like to have a bottle of brandy with me when I travel. It helps with those funny turns I sometimes have – fright!

In the car park outside the Gare Maritime at St Malo I found what I was looking for – a 1972 Dino Ferrari GT. There was a small crowd gathered round it admiring the low, grey aluminium body, fluted and wrought by Pinin Farina in broad, powerful lines. A long-haired French youth was shielding the light from his eyes as he peered through the side window. He announced in an awed voice that the speedometer was marked up to 170 m.p.h. and 270 kilometres an hour.

I had collected the key from the desk in the Gare Maritime where Kerensky's friend had left it for me. The crowd stood back respectfully as I sauntered up, unlocked the door and threw my rucksack on the passenger seat. I hoped I would be able to find reverse in less than five minutes and wouldn't grind the gears. I caught a few whispered insults in French about Week's clothes and eccentric millionaires.

The 2.4 litre Dino looks like a low-slung lunar module. I should not have been surprised to find Neil Armstrong and Buzz Aldrin sitting in there when I opened the door. Luckily the short gear lever was slotted into one of those polished aluminium plates with little canals cut to show where the different gears are. And the positions of reverse and first to fifth were marked clearly on the knob. So I got away from the crowd with an arrogant swirl of tyres and exhaust. The folded *Carte Michelin* I had studied on the hydrofoil was open on the passenger seat beside me. My route was due south to Rennes, turning east to Le Mans along N157 and on through Orléans to hit the great north-south Autoroute beyond Montargis.

I spent the first two hours looking in the mirror for signs of the British or French police and East German SSD men. But all I saw were *camions*, and weekending French families setting out in their saloons for the countryside. The Ferrari hurried along among them, impatient to get at the open road on the Autoroute. Even so I passed through Montargis four hours after leaving St Malo.

I stopped at a Café there to refresh myself before joining the milling Autoroute race track to the south. The French drive every kilometre as if their lives depend on it. Consequently their lives often do. The death wish seems to force the French foot down to the floorboards. And the man at the top of the leg likes to pull out from two feet behind you at right angles, with a swerve like the shake of a tadpole's tail, to overtake. The sight of a foreign car seems to drop a curtain over the last vestige of common sense remaining in his head and he will career wildly about the road, defending France's honour against the invader in a stop-at-nothing endeavour to prove his Gallic manhood and get past.

I knew the Dino would be like a red rag to a bull – so I took only one *pastis* with my black coffee. I spread a whole wheel of Camembert on half a baguette of French bread, wolfed it down and took my rucksack to the lavatory in the back of the café.

Dirty, bespectacled semi-bearded hippy Frank Smith went in – and clear-eyed, business-suited, semi-bearded Jonathan Robson emerged two minutes later with his gardening clothes in the rucksack. I glanced round the noisy café with its lunchtime crowd of wine bibbers. But nobody was looking at the transformed Robson.

In the Dino I unlocked the glove compartment and pulled out a black .45 service revolver. It looked like a war relic belonging to Kerensky's friend – a Webley & Scott with a swivel ring in the butt. I turned it over and snapped it open and got the uneasy feeling that my life would expire the moment it was fired. I had asked Kerensky to get his friend to supply a weapon if he could. I almost wished that he hadn't been able to. It clearly hadn't been fired for years, was dry and ungreased. I think I was right about it being a war relic – but from 1914–18! A box of old ammunition was in the rear of the glove compartment. I hurriedly put them back and locked them away. I didn't like playing with firearms. Or using them seriously come to that. Guns were an acquired taste that I'd never acquired.

As I eased the Ferrari along the steeply-cambered road from Montargis to the Autoroute the tall plane trees at the roadside broke the autumn sunshine into evenly spaced yellow enclosures. As I drove I went back in my mind over the conversation at breakfast with Kerensky.

'The lives of my brother's wife and daughter are paramount,' he said. 'If in your attempt to free them their lives are put at serious risk, you must stop. If it is a choice between them living or dying on the one hand, and removing the threat to the Trust on the other, you must put their lives first,' he said, passing a hand over a grey face that hadn't slept much. He had written out and

63

signed a cheque for a thousand pounds – my retainer – and put it in an envelope addressed to my bank in London. We had posted it on the drive into town.

'Where is the house?' I asked.

'By the end of the Pont St Bénézet.'

'Pity it isn't next to the famous Pont d'Avignon,' I said smiling, 'I could have done a bit of sightseeing at the same time.'

'The Pont St Bénézet *is* the famous Pont d'Avignon,' he said.

'Which end is the house then?' I asked quickly, trying to regain lost ground.

'There is only one end,' Rodica Kerensky cut in. 'The bridge was built in the twelfth century, you know, and some of it has crumbled away. It ends rather suddenly now at the fourth arch in the middle of the river. The house is, not surprisingly, at the end on the bank.'

'Really?' I said, drawing the word out. 'I didn't know that.' I kept my voice bright and innocent. 'I've never been to Avignon before.'

'My brother lives in an old turreted house overlooking the bridge,' Kerensky said. 'It is a very old part of the city. The Palais des Papes where the Popes took refuge from the wars in the fourteenth century is close by. My brother's house is historic and rather austere. Because it was built as a fortified house for a French nobleman it is rather difficult to get into, even today.'

'How do your brother and his family get in normally,' I asked, raising my eyebrows.

'Through the courtyard gate and the front door, of course,' Kerensky said shortly, 'Why do you ask?'

'I might try it as a last resort,' I said.

I could see that Kerensky thought his last resort – me – wasn't a very hopeful one. I had asked a few more questions about the temperament of Madame Croissé and her daughter, the interior of the house and where his brother thought they were being held. I left Kerensky hunched over his coffee looking like an agitated vulture that didn't know where its next cadaver was coming from.

The Dino brightened as the feed-in to the Autoroute slipped

under the tread of its broad Michelin radials. I pulled up at the entry arches to the motorway and slung two franc pieces into the metal *péage* basket. This changed the light from red to green and I spurted through on to the flat runway that has been slashed along the length to France, apparently to allow French drivers every opportunity to try to get their cars airborne.

I was pushing the aluminium Ferrari up to 120 m.p.h. for the first time in fifth when I saw another set of *péage* arches like the starting stalls of a horse racing-track coming towards me fast. I slowed, stopped, took the punched computer card offered me and moved on again with what seemed to be a large proportion of the French nation in big Citroëns, Porsches and Mercedes flying along in front, behind and all around me.

I scurried among the motorized lemmings, quickly falling into the habit of leaning long blasts on the horn and flashing my yellow lights angrily at anyone who dared to pull into the outside lane doing less than 100 m.p.h.

The cars fled on like leaves on the surface of a millrace, hurtling smoothly down towards the southern end of France.

A stiffness of tension in the muscles of my shoulders and an ache behind my eyes reminded me at last I had been fighting the French on their Autoroute for four hour apart from brief cessations of hostility at *péage* toll grids and filling stations. I emerged blinking, at last, from the speed trance and pulled off on to the capillary road into Avignon. I cruised into the outskirts and a large signboard at the side of the road told me modestly I was now entering one of Europe's most historic cities.

I suddenly found myself humming that little tune:

> *Sur le Pont*
> *D'Avignon*
> *On y danse*
> *On y danse*
> *Sur le Pont*
> *D'Avignon*
> *On y danse*
> *Tout en rond.*

I looked at my watch and found it was just after six o'clock. That left me about half an hour of daylight to find the house where the Croissés were held hostage.

Fourteen

I buried the Dino in among the serried ranks of vehicles drawn up in the car park at the end of the Place de L'Horloge. I didn't want a crowd of admirers standing round it if I returned to make a hurried modern departure from one of Europe's most historic cities.

I crossed the Place du Palais, turned into the narrow, cobbled streets of fourteenth-century Avignon and made for the old city ramparts skirting the Quai du Rhône and the river. The crenellated battlements, towers and turrets of the Palace of the Popes frowned down from behind me, dominating Avignon and the Rhône with the same stony, imperious disdain that the Kremlin employs to intimidate Moscow.

In less than five minutes I came upon the Croissé villa. Tall, black, wrought-iron gates guarded a high wall of yellow-white local stone. From the narrow, cobbled street all that was visible above the top of the wall was a high turret at one corner and a roof of faded orange tiles dappled with grey-green moss. The Kerensky family certainly loved their fortifications.

I didn't stare or stop. I walked briskly by, taking in as much as I could with a casual glance. I decided not to cross the road to see if the gates were fastened. They looked as if they were. There was a heavy, iron lock built into the gate next to a pineapple-shaped handle. The front door and shutters on the windows were closed. The Croissés are out of town, the frontage seemed to say.

I hurried on in case East German eyes were peering out. I took the next right turn and went down towards the river.

I came out through the city ramparts just south of the Pont St Bénézet. The bridge juts out into the Rhône like a faded and forgotten jetty of yellowing stone at a point where the river swirls westwards, then turns south again towards the Golfe du Lion. The light was beginning to fade and the four arches hugged their thickening shadows against the polished surface of the water. I could see the abrupt end of the bridge in mid-stream. The yellow stone looked as if it had been severed abruptly by a cheese wire and open water flowed where the consumed section once stood.

At the foot of the bridge a sandwich board stood on the pavement announcing '*Visite du Pont St Bénézet*.' An arrow pointed to what looked like a tiny sweet shop or café. Visits finished at 7 p.m., said the sandwich board. I checked my watch and decided I might invest one franc in the last fifteen minutes before closing time and look at the Croissé villa from the back.

A middle-aged woman in a green overall came out from behind a clutter of *couleurs naturelles* picture postcards, cheap metal souvenirs and guidebooks to the bridge.

'*Vous n'avez pas beaucoup de temps, Monsieur,*' she said, glancing up at the elaborate electric clock encased in a green metal box on the wall.

I smiled and told her I had come a long way to see the bridge today. Ten minutes were better than not seeing it at all, I said, shrugging exaggeratedly as Englishmen always do when speaking French in France. Then I went through the door at the back of the shop and up the stone steps to the bridge.

Ivy climbed up a wall thickly to my left. I turned and hurried out along the ancient cobbled walk of the Pont d'Avignon. I noticed that electric cables ran along the base of the handrails to the chapel bell tower in the middle of the bridge. I guessed the bells were linked to the electric clock in the shop. I waited until I had reached the centre of the *pont* before turning to look back. I leaned against a gate in the railings cutting off the blind end of the bridge to the public '*Il est interdit de franchir cette porte,*' said a sign on it. So I didn't open it.

Through the deepening dusk I could see the round turrets of the Croissé villa and its mossy roof. I saw, too, an unrailed flight of stone steps leading to a door on the second floor. But I dismissed it immediately as a point of entry since there was no chance of its being open, even if it was accessible from the bridge. The courtyard wall was lower at that point and ran close to the steps in a series of right-angled turns. It looked easy enough to climb on to the wall from the bridge.

I looked into the little chapel. A simple stone altar was set at the top of three steps. To the left of the altar five more stone steps led down towards a second chapel built into the bridge underneath. But from the bottom step to the floor of the lower chapel was a drop of some thirteen feet.

I went quickly back to the little shop. The woman in the green overall closed the door behind me as the mechanism in the electric clock on the wall began to whirr. I walked to the gate in the ramparts, with the two bells in the belfry above the bridge chapel clamouring seven o'clock.

I headed for the Place de L'Horloge again, wondering why I had ever thought I could winkle three armed Communists and two hostages out of a private house in Avignon. The thought of a hundred and fifty thousand pounds had obviously gone to my head. No Errol Flynn inspiration had arrived so far, either.

Lights were coming on in the square. French soldiers from a nearby camp were thick among the evening crowds. They sat outside the pavement restaurants wearing khaki uniforms and those big floppy black berets with coloured tufts. A cool mistral, blowing from the *golfe*, was stirring the yellowing leaves of the plane trees.

I strolled through the paved centre of the square, considering how the Army would go about entering the Croissé villa and freeing the mother and daughter.

Students were composing lurid pictures in coloured chalks on the paving stones beneath the trees. Beside them they wrote legends like '*Aidez nous à nourir un petit chat*'. And appended white chalk hearts with '*Merci*' written underneath to receive the stroller's coins. Nobody seemed to have been moved to help them feed any little cats so far. All the hearts were empty.

Among the dappled, peeling trunks of the plane trees, cane chairs and tables were set out covered with paper table-cloths. Waiters dashed back and forth through the busy evening traffic from the restaurants on the far side of the road to feed those sitting in the centre of the square. The sight and smell of the food reminded me that condemned men were supposed to eat heartily to show they weren't afraid. So I sat down with my back to the *horloge* on the front of the Hôtel de Ville which gave the square its name and tried to impress the waiters by ordering steak and *pommes frites* in a voice steeled with courage.

I found myself wishing a battalion of the fresh-faced young soldiers sitting around the square in ones and twos might come to my table to offer their combat strength *en masse*. Swear to stay at my side for the night's assault on the Villa Croissé, that sort of thing. But they didn't. And I couldn't eat heartily. So I paid my bill and took my change across the square towards the river and the Croissé villa.

The narrow cobbled street was deserted. I moved along it almost on tip-toe. Seventy yards short of the house I froze. The creak and groan of the wrought-iron gate being swung open carried to me an instant before the figure of a man emerged from the shadow of the gateway. In that instant I stepped into an archway.

After glancing in both directions the man hurried away along the street. He didn't look round again.

I stayed in the shelter of the arch until he had been out of sight for two minutes. Then I stepped back on to the narrow pavement and walked quickly towards the Villa Croissé.

I knew now the way was open. He hadn't locked the gates behind him.

Fifteen

As I walked the end of the barrel of the Webley & Scott war relic dug into that soft gully that runs along the top of the thigh to the hip. I'd tucked it into the waistband of my trousers because the Ever Ready rubber torch already filled the pocket inside the left lapel of my jacket. So I walked quickly but with a slight, limping roll of the left leg to minimize the penetration of the barrel and its front sight. I didn't like to ease the revolver upwards in case it fell out with a clatter on the pavement. Errol wouldn't have been proud of his shambling, clumsily-armed, latter-day protégé.

I twisted the iron pineapple and pushed hard on the gate. It swung open noisily on unoiled hinges. I closed it just as noisily and stepped quickly up to the steps leading to the front door.

The house was in darkness. By the light from the street I could see a smaller iron pineapple poking out from a circular mounting beside the heavy double doors. The top step of the porch was paved in large black and white chessboard squares. I shifted my feet so that they fitted neatly into the squares, right foot into a black one, left in a white one. I didn't want to get the whole thing off to an unlucky start by standing on the cracks.

I took hold of the little black pineapple and pulled. This was rewarded by a subdued pealing of bells. I looked up at the antique windowed lantern hanging from a hook in the roof of the porch. I hoped it wouldn't come on before the door was opened – if it was opened.

Two minutes passed without any sound. I was reaching for the bell pull again when I heard a soft football on the other side of the door.

'*Qui est là?*' The voice, asking who was there, was guttural and uneasy with the French words. The door hadn't opened. No bolts or locks had shifted. No light had come on.

'*Ich komme gerade aus der Normannen Strasse!*' I said, mentioning the street where the SSD headquarters stand in East Berlin. '*Es gibt etwas ganz Neues. Hartmann und Klaus haben grosse Schwierigkeiten in Jersey gehabt.*'

I had leaned close to the door to make myself heard, piling on the Berlin Cockney accent for all it was worth – which probably wasn't much.

There was silence for a moment, while the man on the other side of the door considered whether he cared about the undefined troubles Hartmann and Klaus were allegedly having in Jersey. I hoped that their job had been mounted on the basis of a telephone silence. If there had been any contact between the Villa Croissé and East Berlin I was already making a fool of myself. They would know I was a bogus messenger.

Then a lock clicked and a bolt scraped and the door swung open a foot. Nothing was revealed except a shadow, two inches wide.

'*Vogel,*' I said sticking my hand into the shadow. '*Darf ich 'rein?*'

70

A hand shook that of Herr Vogel that I had stuck in the door.

'*Schwarz. Bitte, hereinkommen.*' The shadow spoke, identified itself and invited me in.

It was pitch black inside when the door closed behind me. I tried the Berlin-accented German again – it was almost as good as whistling in the darkness of the hall.

'Which way? Up here?'

I could see a sliver of light escaping under a door at the top of the double staircase and started for it. I stumbled against the bottom step. Speaking over my shoulder, I made a vulgar suggestion as to how I thought the time was being passed guarding two French women in a house with all the lights out.

A grunt was all I got from Herr Schwarz. He pressed dourly up the stairs behind me. Either he had no sense of humour or he didn't want to spoil the aim of the pistol which he had just pushed against my bottom rib.

Maybe he was just being cautious – as he was trained to be. Or I had already committed some obvious blunder. I remembered now my Berlin friends had often told me that my talent for mimicking accents wasn't as good as I thought myself.

Light coming under the door at the top of the stairs was now about level with my head. My eyes were getting accustomed to the dark. I could see that the landing was tiled with big black and white squares like the front porch. That meant there were about six steps to go before we reached a light switch, before the hostage-takers got a good look at me.

I decided that now was the time for something more positive than just stepping over cracks in the floor.

'*Was gibt's mit diesem Revolver?*' I asked over my shoulder in an injured tone. But I didn't wait for him to tell me why he was sticking it in my back. I had quietly pulled the ancient firing piece of Kerensky's friend from my waistband as I spoke.

I lunged abruptly to the left, turning the revolver in my hand until I gripped it by the barrel and trigger guard. Then I swung round and chopped hard down at where I thought Schwarz's head was. The flat of the butt caught him heavily where his parting might have been. He grunted, swayed and crumpled forward. His gun clattered down the stairs.

I turned, tripped, caught myself with my left hand on the banister, stumbled up the last five steps, flung the door back on its hinges and fired two deafening shots straight ahead of me into a smirking, bewigged portrait of Louis XV hanging in a gilded frame on the wall opposite the door.

The shirt-sleeved East German lounging on a long, blue brocade sofa sat up suddenly, thunderstruck. He was only a little more shocked and startled by the deafening roar of the shots than I was. He stared at me transfixed.

Only Louis Quinze was unmoved. He went on smirking under his wig in the golden frame, oblivious of the bullet holes that had enlarged his left nostril and given him a hollow eye socket.

I had fired the shots for their shock effect, calculating that the thick walls of the old house and its retaining courtyard wall would muffle them from the street. As the shock wore off I saw the East German flick his eyes to a nearby chair over which he had slung his jacket – and more foolishly his strapped holster with its pistol fitted snugly in it.

The pungent cordite fumes from the old ammunition curled out of the barrel of the .45 making my eyes smart. But I held it steadily in the East German's direction. I looked towards his jacket and pistol and shook my head meaningfully.

He glanced uneasily towards the door leading into the next room answering my first question wordlessly.

'Madame Croissé,' I yelled in French. 'Are you in there? I am a friend come to help you. From George and Rodica.'

After a long wait a frightened, tremulous '*Oui*' came from the other side of the door.

'*Stillstehen!*' I told the German.

His taut, pale face was gaunt under the bright light of the crystal chandelier suspended from the high ceiling of the drawing-room. His eyes narrowed as he desperately sought some way of retrieving a situation in which he had been caught off guard.

I crossed quickly to the door of the adjoining room, still facing the man on the sofa. The key was in the lock on my side. I turned my back to the door, and continued to face the East German who had twisted to watch me as I passed in front of him.

I called through the door again. 'Madame Croissé, is your daughter with you?'

Again the frightened voice took a long time to reply.

'*Oui*.'

'Listen carefully,' I said, talking over my shoulder. 'Do exactly as I tell you and you will be quite safe. The house is surrounded by *gendarmes*. But first I must get you clear of these men who are still in the house and armed.'

The eyes of the man on the sofa widened with a hint of panic when I mentioned the word *gendarmes*.

Still facing him, I shouted again in French: 'Please prepare to come out of the room, Madame. I shall unlock the door in a moment. Please walk out slowly, both of you. Go to the door to the hall and wait there. Do not look at me or anybody else in the room. Do not walk between us. When you come through the door stay behind me, then walk round the edge of the room. Do you understand? Both of you?'

This time the nervous '*Oui*' had an echo, presumably from the daughter.

'I am unlocking the door now,' I said. 'Take things gently. Everything will be all right.' I managed to get more confidence into my voice than I felt. Then I fumbled behind my back and turned the key.

I took two steps forward away from the door. This brought the distance between me and the German to about ten feet. He watched me intently, his body arched and tensed in an uncomfortable sitting position on the sofa.

The door handle turned behind me and I heard the door ease open. I wondered immediately whether I was the stupidest hostage rescuer of all time. Was there a guard inside the room with them? This might account for their barely-audible, petrified answers.

The German stiffened abruptly and stared past my right ear at the doorway as if sensing my sudden unease.

'*Schnell, Hans!*' he yelled, jerking his body forward in the sitting position, willing his unseen partner to attack.

I gritted my teeth together, tensed muscles in my legs and neck that were urging me to jump and turn round. I remained absolutely motionless with the gun held before me pointing towards the man on the blue sofa. The hair on the back of my neck crawled upright as I waited for a blow.

The gate had creaked and a figure of a man had come out and hurried off along the street, I told myself as the moments dragged slowly by. Croissé had said by phone there were three men. This should have left two in the house. Could they have increased the number of guards from three to four since Croissé phoned from Lyon?

'*Hans! Jetz! Shnell, schnell!*' the man on the sofa screamed again.

There was a movement in the doorway behind me. My hand began to shake.

Then I had an impression from the side of my eye of a grey-blue head moving out and along the wall. Another darker head with longer hair followed. As they turned to skirt the fireplace the heads showed themselves to have bodies dressed in trousers and sweaters. They moved into the front of my vision.

The mother and daughter, shuffling like sleep-walking zombies in front of the hearth, were reflected in the large mirror of decorated Venetian glass above it. They stared straight ahead, obeying my instructions not to look the nightmare they were living in the face.

Nobody else came from the room.

The face of the East German crumpled and he cursed — something elaborate to do with a particularly obscene form of *Schweinhund*.

'Are they still showing those old Hollywood gangster movies in the Normannen Strasse rest room then?' I asked the German with exaggerated incredulity. 'You'll have to learn some newer tricks than that. Or prevent your colleagues from slipping away to decadent bourgeois pleasures in naughty Avignon.'

The French woman and her daughter had reached the door and stopped obediently, staring at the wall.

'Well done, Madame Croissé,' I said switching to French, 'please wait a moment more.'

'Turn round, you,' I told the German.

74

As he turned I moved up behind him. Leaning down towards the sofa I brought the .45 over in an arc towards a point behind his right ear.

I was beginning to feel in practice at hitting people with blunt instruments. I was over-confident.

The German sensed what was coming and was starting to duck his head before the impact. The glancing blow with the butt and swivel ring only cut his forehead and stunned him.

He rolled to the floor in the same instant that the front-door bell jangled in the hall below.

I ran to the two terrified women and hustled them into the corridor.

'The *gendarmes* have arrived, *non*?' said Madame Croissé, turning a face to me that had probably aged five years in two days.

'No!' Which way to the back door with the stone steps outside?' I asked urgently, pushing them along the corridor away from the double staircase and the front hall where Hans was again pealing the bells.

The mother and daughter were making breathless whimpering noises as we went down the back stairs in a scrambling jumble of feet and legs.

'*Voilà!*' Madame Croissé pointed a trembling hand towards a heavy oak door at the bottom of the stone staircase. 'But we have not used it for some years!'

I wrestled unsuccessfully with the heavy key in the rusty lock. Then I heard the front door open and bang and the sound of Hans's feet running up the front stairs. He had obviously tired of ringing and had resorted to an emergency key. In the room at the top of the stairs the dazed voice of the other East German was telling what had happened.

The rusty lock suddenly gave and I pushed the Croissés outside.

'*Où sont les gendarmes, Monsieur?*' the daughter asked, looking round wildly for the French police. Her voice was desperate, pathetic.

'*Je regrette . . .*' I began to say, then decided there was no time for talking. Instead I urged them down the unrailed steps.

75

The outline of the ancient Pont d'Avignon with its curved arches and chapel bell tower was clearly visible against the dark river in the light of the moon. The modern floodlights, reflected from the Palais des Papes inside the city ramparts, added their embarrassing brightness, showing the bridge stopping in mid-stream, its job half done. Another flight of steps led up to the top of the courtyard wall.

I made a quick decision.

'Take these steps, please,' I whispered fiercely. 'We can climb over on to the bridge and be safe there.'

I winced as I dug the .45 back into my waistband – and my groin. I grabbed Madame Croissé close under her left armpit and hustled her up the steps to the top of the courtyard wall. Her daughter followed.

I jumped the five feet from the courtyard wall to the steps leading down to the bridge. Then I reached up and helped the Croissés down. I ushered them forward and down again and we reached the uneven, cobbled surface of the bridge moving in an untidy gaggle. I felt like a sheepdog trying to bring in a couple of winded, nervous strays as we headed out along the Pont d'Avignon towards the shelter of the little chapel.

A square of light suddenly opened up in the dark shadow of the building behind us. Over my shoulder I saw the silhouette of two men emerging from the rear door of the villa.

The square of light disappeared; the door slammed. The shadows moved down the unrailed steps in pursuit.

Sixteen

Madame Croissé, who I guessed was in her fifties, was catching her breath in low sobbing gasps. Climbing and running clearly weren't her usual pastimes. Her teenage daughter was doing a little better. Luckily Madame was making so much noise that my own gasping wasn't as audible as it might have been. Climbing and running had been a long way down my list of leisure priorities, too, in the last few years.

I hauled the rubber torch from my inside pocket and flashed it on the steps twenty yards short of the bell tower. They led down the outer wall of the bridge to the lower chapel.

We helter-skeltered down again. I made comforting noises with a bad French accent as I called a halt in the echoing stone vault. I flashed the torch round the bare, grey slabs of the walls. Three steps led to the simple altar – a single wedge of stone resting on a thick central pillar like a granite mushroom.

'Behind there!' I said pointing and pushing them up the steps. 'Crouch behind the altar and keep your heads down.'

I looked at my watch by the shaded light of my torch. Four minutes to nine.

Three archways led out on to a railed triangular platform that jutted into the river like the pointed prow of a small boat sailing downstream. The moonlight and the reflected floodlights from the Palais des Papes lit the interior of the chapel dimly. Headlights of cars rose smoothly across the next bridge downstream, heading for Nîmes.

Our laboured breathing was the only sound in the tiny chapel. I flashed my torch up to the roof. I remembered, from my visit a few hours before, the eight-foot-long hole in the chapel floor above, its five truncated steps and the thirteen-foot drop to the floor on which we now stood. I could see by the torchlight that a handrail guarded the upper side of the coffin-shaped hole.

I switched the torch off and listened as the footsteps of the East Germans clattered nearer on the cobbles. I hissed for the Croissés to quieten their breathing. The footsteps slowed and stopped outside the upper chapel. I backed against the wall out of direct line with the coffin-shaped hole.

A few muttered words of German were exchanged – but too quietly for me to hear what was said. A torch flashed, probing the dark corners of the stone chamber above our heads.

I doubted whether the Germans had spent sightseeing time on the bridge before mounting their hostage-taking operation. So I hoped my newly-gained knowledge of its lay-out might give me some advantage. Using the gun in my waistband seemed utterly out of the question since the noise of its discharge would be amplified by the echo chamber of the vault-like chapel. And crowds would come running.

With a start I saw that the Germans didn't have that problem. The torchlight was still flicking round the upper chapel and against it the unmistakable, bulbous silhouette of a silenced pistol came slowly into view over the rail guarding the coffin-shaped hole. It moved slowly back and forth like the blind antenna of some enormous insect seeking to pick up the vibrations of its prey in the ancient crypts.

Then I heard the other German coming down the steps on the outer wall of the bridge. He came slowly and carefully, stopping every two steps to listen.

The man above my head was moving too. The rustle of his clothing and the squeak of grit beneath his soles told me he had eased over the protecting rail and was crouching on the bottom of the five steps. Ready to pump his silenced bullets into any corner of the cellar chapel – or ready to plummet down the thirteen feet to join us.

I wondered if it were Hans above my head or his partner, thirsting to revenge the humiliation I had inflicted on him on that brocade-covered sofa.

The man on the outer steps was on his toes now, making his footsteps barely audible as he came down the last few feet. He wanted to close the pincer on us as quietly as possible.

A whinny of nervous hysteria came from behind the altar. It was followed by the louder sound of the daughter hushing her mother.

That was goodbye to the last chance of surprise we had through our concealment.

'There is no way out for you.'

The voice came softly from around the wall at the foot of the outer steps. The English was accented, but good.

'Throw all your weapons into the middle of the floor and come out with your hands on your heads. That way nobody will get hurt.'

Through the triple archways car headlights still showed themselves downriver, darting across the bridge towards Nîmes. The shallow Rhône gurgled heedlessly round the medieval piles of the Pont d'Avignon as it had done for eight hundred years.

Inside the chapel in the bowels of the bridge there was absolute silence. Five people were holding their breath simultaneously. The East Germans were sure of the prey now. But they weren't going to rush the *coup de grâce*.

Grit squeaked again under the soles of the shoes on the truncated staircase above my head. I had the Ever Ready torch in one hand and Messrs Webley & Scott's .45 in the other, backed up against the wall, trying to look two ways at once in the semi-darkness.

The one sensible thing to do in a situation like this was to panic. Only the ear-shuddering crash and clang of colliding metal that rocked the darkened chapel without warning prevented me.

As the bells in the tower above boomed a second time, marking the hour on the orders of the electric clock in the little souvenir shop, I added the unhealthy roar of the .45 to the din.

I switched on my torch and swung it quickly up into the coffin-shaped recess above me. The beam revealed the knees, feet and hands of the man crouching there with the silenced pistol. The overhang prevented him seeing me. I was beneath and behind him.

I stretched out the .45 at arm's length, gritted my teeth, half closed my eyes and fired twice at his knees from about ten-feet range. The gun bucked in my hand; there was a shout of pain from above. I switched off the torch quickly and dodged bent double to a new position.

In the darkness the man fell heavily through the hole in the thick floor above, knocking against its sides as he came. He hit the stone flags a few feet from me. The sickening thud and the loose flopping of his limbs and head were clearly audible between the booming strokes of the hour from the bells. Then he lay still.

'Hans?'

The voice from the outer staircase called the frantic question, '*Bist du OK?*'

This time I recognized the voice. It was the man from the brocade sofa again. He was clearly not enjoying his evening. Or the support he was getting from his comrades.

'Hans has fallen out with you,' I called towards the bottom of the steps. Then under cover of the ninth stroke of the bells I loosed a sloppy shot in the vague direction of the steps.

As the sound of the bells died away, whimpering became audible again from behind the altar. So did the sound of the German's feet racing back up the steps. He seemed to have decided to cut his losses.

'Stay where you are,' I snapped at the Croissés and took the steps two at a time.

The East German in his panic turned right at the top of the steps and ran out along the bridge. He seemed to have forgotten it didn't reach the other side of the Rhône. I pounded after him, stumbling on the uneven cobbles. He swung open the gate in the railings ignoring the sign that said it was '*interdit de franchir cette porte*' and ran on.

He threw a bewildered glance over his shoulder when he began to realize something was wrong with the narrow roadway that had been built to transport horses and twelfth-century pedestrians across the Rhône.

Then he jerked to a halt a few feet from the severed end of the bridge. He had realized finally that it would not carry a twentieth-century Communist agent to the far bank.

He turned as I came up. I didn't know what I wanted to do except eliminate the final threat to my getting the Croissés safely out of Avignon.

I hurled the rubber Ever Ready at his head from a distance of about six feet. He flung up his arms and tried to duck at the same moment. His feet slithered on the loose stones and gravel of the crumbling bridge-end. Then he lost his balance and fell sideways.

There was no sound until the heavy splash.

I stood staring over the abrupt precipice for a second, breathing hard. I didn't go to the edge to look down in case I slipped, myself. Then I remembered I had left the Croissés alone. I raced back and down the steps calling assurances ahead of me. They still cowered behind the altar and the man on the flagstones hadn't moved.

I dropped the .45 into my inside pocket. Trying to comfort the hysterical Madame Croissé, I moved them rapidly up to the top level of the bridge and back to the eastern bank. I found a way out through some loose boards in a fence behind the little souvenir shop.

In the back of a café in the city ramparts a quarter of a mile from the bridge I put my jacket round Madame Croissé. I told her not to try to talk until she had drunk the large Cognac I ordered for her. I ordered another for the daughter and one for myself. After gulping it down I went to the door and looked back towards the bridge.

It still stood.

And it looked as if it might go on standing for another eight hundred years. I heard no police sirens, saw no cars or groups of excited onlookers. It seemed as if Avignon and its bridge hadn't noticed anything unusual.

So I went back into the café and ordered three more Cognacs.

Seventeen

'You were *fantastique*!'

I looked over the rim of my Cognac glass at Madame Croissé's daughter whose name was Jeannine. She spoke schoolgirl English. I guessed she was about seventeen.

I grinned at her, agreed that I thought I'd been pretty '*fantastique*' too, then asked her mother how she was feeling now. She shrugged, but said nothing. She wasn't capable of words yet.

Her hands were still shaking slightly as she held them both to the Cognac glass before her on the table. Some of the shock was thawing from a face that had been beautiful in its youth. The haggard lines of fear were softening.

She still darted furtive glances over my shoulder to the door from time to time. The nightmare of being held under armed guard in her own familiar and comfortable house with its luxurious trappings, clearly had not entirely left her yet. It probably wouldn't for a few hours, or maybe days.

After a while she asked after her husband, with a touch of asperity as if she felt he had run out on them. She asked, too, about George and Rodica Kerensky. But it was not hard to detect an underlying acidity in her tone. Her inquiry was interested, as she realized their fortunes were bound together, but without affection.

I thought I began to see why grandfather Kerensky had gone to such elaborate lengths to set up his three-cornered trust. There seemed to me to be little love lost between the Kerensky brothers, although I knew nothing yet of the one who lived in Switzerland.

Madame Croissé was looking nervously over my shoulder again to the door.

'I don't think there will be any more trouble from our friends,' I said soothingly. 'Their ranks are fairly well depleted now and I doubt whether they would be prepared to try anything foolish in full view of the population of Avignon!'

I tried to get hot-water-bottle-and-warm-milk comfort into the broad smile I gave her. Then I added the bad news.

'I'm afraid we have got to set off fairly soon to drive five hundred miles in a two-seater car – and drive fast. Those men don't wish to harm you for harm's sake. But I think it would be safer if you were completely beyond their reach. So there is no chance of you being used to put pressure on the Trust. We're leaving for Jersey – now.'

I explained what the East Germans had been trying to do. I noticed as I spoke that Jeannine was staring at me with wide eyes. She had full, palely-pink unpainted lips, that pushed forward in a permanent Brigitte Bardot pout. Her black sweater of corded wool stretched tight over slim shoulders and arms – so tight that it was clear she wasn't wearing anything underneath. She tilted her chin whenever she spoke, constantly tossing her long, dark hair back from her face. And she looked around archly to check the effect this was having.

Her youthful resilience was already enabling her to turn the horror of the past two days into a drama in which she had played the role of the heroine. She had become flushed and animated with release and the Cognac.

'But you reely were *fantastique*,' she said again, looking at me from under her lowered lashes as she sipped her drink. 'Ze way you took command of ze situation ... and rescued us. *Merveilleux!*'

She smiled straight into my eyes the way she had seen somebody do it in the Avignon Odeon — or whatever they called their main cinema. She wanted to be found attractive by the hero. 'And you know? You look a leetle bit like Roger Vadim,' she said, tossing her hair back again and breathing deeply until the black corded sweater swelled. She took a quick look round.

I got the impression she was checking to see that Vadim wasn't creeping up with his camera at that moment to discover her. Her expression indicated she believed fervently that sooner or later Roger Vadim *would* discover her — and she kept the pout permanently in place so she wouldn't be caught unawares when he did eventually come through the door.

I gave her a twisted, underplayed Jean Gabin smile, said nothing and lit a cigarette.

I blew smoke to the ceiling then said in French: 'We must get on the road to St Malo soon. Either you will have to sit very uncomfortably on each other's laps or ...' I let my gaze run down the black sweater. 'Or you, Jeannine, since you are young and slim, could try to curl up behind the seats. Either way it won't be comfortable.'

Jeannine wriggled in her seat and pulled a *gamine* face at me without her mother seeing. Madame Croissé ran a hand heavy with rings — most of them diamonds — over her blue-grey hair. I could see now it was rinsed. She shrugged and sighed loudly. The Cognacs were numbing the shock, if not removing it completely. She looked out from eyes with heavy blue circles beneath them and said: 'I am prepared. Shall we go?'

I left some notes on the table and walked them quickly towards the Place du Palais and the Dino Ferrari, holding each by the elbow.

'What 'appened to ze man 'oo fell off ze bridge?' Jeannine asked, looking up at me round-eyed. She seemed determined to exercise her English.

'I don't know. But he can probably swim and he'll have found his way to the bank by now.'

'And ze osser one at ze top of our stairs?'

'I think he'll come round eventually, too. And if he's got any sense he'll get out of your house quickly, closing the doors behind him.'

I increased my pace at the thought of the two men. 'Perhaps they will go up to the chapel on the bridge and take care of their friend. Otherwise he may provide an unexpected sight when the bridge opens to sightseers in the morning.'

I spotted the grey Dino glimmering expensively in the reflected light from the Auberge de France near the side of the square. I unlocked the passenger's door. I pushed the seats forward as far as they would go and helped Jeannine squeeze into the narrow space behind them. She pushed the front of the black sweater coquettishly against my shirt and tie as she eased by into the car.

But I was not paying her much attention. Across the top of the Dino I could see into the lighted hall of the *auberge*. One of the few people in Avignon that I knew was just finishing a telephone call at the public call box there. As I bent to help Madame Croissé into the front seat he turned and looked at me across the low roof of the car. For the third time that night the man from the brocade sofa and I exchanged hostile stares. He wore a dry raincoat over his wet suit and his hair was tousled and damp.

I ran round to the driver's door and jumped in. I started the engine, swept the car into reverse, pulled back, moved into first and shot out of the parking area.

I glanced up and saw the brocade-sofa man in my driving mirror. He stood staring for a moment. Then he turned back into the café again, towards the phone.

I drove quickly out of Avignon without mentioning what I had seen to my passengers.

Eighteen

By midnight I was quietly cursing the builders of France's Autoroute for taking it through the cluttered, grimy centre of Lyon instead of round it. The Rhône, which had wandered away in its valley to our left as we fled northward from Avignon, had now swung back under the road to lie dark, viscous and urban on our right.

I started cursing again as I stopped at the ninth traffic light since entering the outskirts of Lyon ten minutes earlier.

Madame Croissé dozed fitfully beside me. She still had my jacket pulled close round her. The journey from Avignon had been uneventful – if you didn't count further contributions to the French revenue at two *péage* toll grids – and Jeannine winding her fingers quietly into the hair on the back of my neck.

She had coiled herself into an uncomfortable prone position behind us. The space behind the Dino's seats was minimal even with the passenger seat and my driving seat as far forward on their frames as they would go. This meant I was driving with my knees up under my chin. Jeannine was lying on one hip with her knees behind her mother. The Dino's choke is between and behind the seats and from time to time she emitted little squeals and groans and complained petulantly about the choke lever bruising her.

When she tired of this she rested her chin and arms on the back of my seat. To amuse herself in a manner befitting one of Vadim's future girls she let her breath out surreptitiously through pouted lips to play gently on the lobe of my right ear. And twisted a curling piece of hair between her fingers. Whenever her mother turned to her she stopped and answered her question with exaggerated child-like innocence.

Vadim, she clearly thought, would have been pleased with any heroine who managed to arouse the hero in her mother's presence without her realizing it.

I had stared stolidly ahead through the windscreen at the twin floods of yellow light pointing our way north up the Autoroute and ignored her. At 125 m.p.h. the eyes fix themselves ahead in a rigid, instinctive discipline imposed by the reflexes of survival.

The twisted road through Lyon was straightening itself now and levelling out once more into the wide runways of the Autoroute. I accelerated.

I was beginning to congratulate myself on putting the danger of pursuit safely behind us. I yawned long and loud for the second time in five minutes. It seemed a week had passed since those four hours of sleep in the Kerensky farmhouse in Jersey. And it would be several hours more yet. I was aiming to reach St Malo in time to catch the nine-thirty hydrofoil back to the island.

I noticed that the French had added their own distinctive touch to the featureless, supra-national motorway tracks. Young poplars planted in between the north and south lanes were growing into a green fence that already eased the strain of high-speed traffic streaming from the opposite direction with headlights flaring.

I yawned again. 'At the next Jacques Borel restaurant we'll stop for some *café au lait*,' I said, breaking a long silence.

In the dim reflection of the dashboard panel lights I could see Madame Croissé nodding dumbly. Behind me I could feel Jeannine easing herself into a new position of discomfort.

The white Mercedes 350 SLC parked on the hard shoulder of the road by a breakdown telephone kiosk caught my attention as the Dino's headlights picked it out. My first instinct was to slow down when the man in hat and coat standing beside it stepped to the edge of the road and waved his arm in the perpendicular, slow-down sign. Then I changed my mind and spurted past. The road was by no means deserted and if he was in trouble, let somebody else help.

But there was nothing wrong with the Mercedes. I had slowed to around 75 m.p.h. before deciding against stopping. As I plunged down on the accelerator again I caught the reflection in my mirror of the Mercedes parked at an oblique angle to the road. The man in the hat and coat had jumped back in the car. The Ferrari was running through the long yellow tunnel of the Mercedes' headlamps. But they were no longer stationary. The white car was no longer in need of the breakdown telephone.

A large blue board with white lettering came quickly towards us announcing an outlet to Villefranche-sur-Saône. Another glance in the mirror showed that the Mercedes' headlights were moving fast as it built up speed quickly from standstill.

I found it hard to believe that the East Germans in Avignon could have such a well-equipped back-up group in Lyon. But there was the white Mercedes driving hard behind me.

I toyed with the idea of going off towards Villefranche. The Mercedes' 3.5 litre V8 engine would make it difficult to shake off on the Autoroute. Then I decided there was less likelihood of getting forced into a corner on the big road.

The noise of the wind rushing over the polished surfaces of the Ferrari began to build up as I forced it towards its top speed in fifth. I swung out round a *camion* that shouldn't have been driving at that time on Sunday morning and stayed in the fast lane.

Madame Croissé sat forward in her seat. I guessed that a look of alarm was returning to the face that had been relaxed in sleep moments before.

'Must we drive so fast?' she asked plaintively in French. 'Is anything wrong?' The second question was more urgent. She'd probably caught sight of my set face staring up the road.

Jeannine began to grip the back of my seat as the rear-mounted engine growled upwards to a high-speed roar.

'Qu'est-ce que c'est?' she said frantically. The play acting and English practice had stopped now. The sense of danger made it evaporate as quickly as it had come in the Avignon café.

'I think we're being followed. Chased, if you like,' I said shortly in French. I was angry with the Croissés. Their presence in the car was responsible for the danger and I was tired.

The glare of the Mercedes' undipped lights through the back window threw our three shadows forward inside the Ferrari. The needle on the speedometer crept up waveringly between 135 and 140 m.p.h.

The Autoroute mixes long fast curves with straight stretches. The road ahead was empty and I hugged the nearside up a long gradient. The Mercedes flew along on station a quarter of a mile back. The distance between the cars hadn't changed. I was hanging on to my start but I couldn't lengthen it. After ten minutes of this my hands were damp on the wheel and my mouth was dry.

A downhill stretch with a left-hand turn barriered and decorated with *Virages* warning signs loomed ahead. I drove hard into the outside lane, braked, and accelerated across to the inside of the bend trying to straighten it and keep the speedometer over the hundred. The Ferrari juddered into a sideways slide towards the barrier. But it finally righted itself with the nearside wheels already on the hard shoulder and ran on downhill.

Driving with my knees under my chin obviously wasn't good for control at high speed.

The tyres of the Mercedes screamed behind as its driver brought it down and through the bend faster and better than I'd dared. At the bottom of the hill the Autoroute straightened to climb slowly over a long, broad hill.

I looked in the mirror. The Mercedes seemed to have halved the distance between us.

Nineteen

From the corner of my eye I could see Madame Croissé sitting white-faced and tense, clutching the sides of her seat. The pallid face of her daughter jerked in and out of my vision in the driving mirror as she struggled in the confined space behind me in the hurtling car. I expect my own made the total three white faces in the Ferrari.

'Who is chasing us?' gasped Madame Croissé, half turning in her seat.

'I don't know. But I'm not proposing to stop to find out,' I replied through gritted teeth. 'Friends of your house guests, perhaps. After the toothbrush they left in the bathroom.'

The Mercedes was about a hundred and fifty yards behind now.

Fine points of rain began to speckle the windscreen. They grew larger and I turned on the fast wipers. Then I leaned forward suddenly to peer ahead through the rain. Lights were strung across the road about a mile ahead. A blue board flashed by on our right.

'*Péage à 1000 mètres*,' it said.

I checked the mirror and eased my foot off the accelerator. The Mercedes closed to twenty yards.

This seemed to be another good time to panic.

For a foolish moment I wondered whether to try to crash through the *péage* toll gates. If I stopped would the car behind unload a bevy of gunmen who would stick pistols in the faces

88

of the *péage* officials and hold them at gunpoint while they abducted us? Wouldn't getting caught like that be worse than smashing through, splintering barriers and setting off lights and alarms and running, shouting men?

I didn't know how many men were in the car behind. It could hold four or five but I had only seen the driver.

I slowed down, and leaned across, holding my computer card with a ten-franc note out of the passenger window towards the control box. I had decided to count on those in the car behind not wanting to work under the public gaze.

As the toll man took my money I heard the Mercedes draw up behind. The driver's window wound down.

'Stop, damn you! I've something new from London!' the driver shouted in a rounded English accent – or a good imitation of one.

'I've already used that one myself today, sweetheart – in German,' I called back over my shoulder.

Then I let in the clutch and shot away.

I got up about a hundred fifty yards by flattening the accelerator to the boards first, second and third before the Mercedes paid and came away from the *péage*.

'*Bon dieu!* Why didn't you stop?' Madame Croissé demanded in French. 'He's a friend, isn't he? He spoke English.'

'That's exactly how I got into your house,' I told her wearily. 'By pretending to bring news of a late development from Berlin. With a *German* accent.'

The fast two-car parade was on again. After another five minutes the better driving of the man in the Mercedes through two fast left-hand bends had brought him up to within fifty yards. I wished I was keener on driving at 130 m.p.h. And better at it with my chin on my knees in a right-hand-drive car on left-hand-drive roads.

Big blue boards for Mâcon were beginning to appear in the headlights now. I began to feel the headlong dash could go on for ever – until we ran out of road east of Calais and splashed into the Channel ducking and draking at over 100 m.p.h.

But the driver behind clearly didn't wish to leave the issue unresolved that long. The Mercedes had crammed on all its speed as we went round to the right up a steep gradient. Then the headlights flared in my mirror as it began to close fast on the outside. I accelerated hard, but the big white car crept nearer.

It began to edge alongside in the overtaking position. I hauled the steering wheel of the Ferrari over and placed myself squarely in front of it in the outside lane. Madame Croissé's hands flew to her face with a little cry. The Mercedes braked sharply, fell back twenty yards, then started to come again – on my inside this time.

The three-pointed star on its bonnet crept along until it was level with the door handle by my elbow. I realized I had left it too late to pull over in front again.

The needle of the speedometer danced on 138 m.p.h.

The Mercedes' star nosed ahead and the yelling face of its driver indicated through our two rolled-up windows that I should pull over. He edged the sharp, white wing of the Mercedes nearer to the bonnet of the Dino to emphasize his demand. His car was a left-hand drive so we sat side by side at a shuddering 140 m.p.h.

A screen of eight-foot-tall poplars ran close on the left of the Dino up the middle of the road. I eased back to a hundred, then ninety. I looked sideways at the yelling face behind the glass in the Mercedes and nodded.

Then as he narrowed in ahead to restrict my path further between him and the young trees I shouted a warning to my passengers.

'Madame, Jeannine! Brace yourselves! Hold tight to the seats!'

I swung the nose of the Ferrari hard to the left.

Two young poplars went flat under the bonnet. The car burst through, bucked, jumped, then slammed its four wheels hard back on the road dragging a poplar tree caught in the chassis. Madame Croissé was flung forward to strain against the limit of her seat belt. The glare of oncoming lights flooded through the windscreen blinding me.

I hauled the wheel back towards the middle line of poplars. The glare disappeared. The Ferrari skidded, straightened, then settled square, running fast down the wrong side of the Autoroute. The dragging poplar fell away. The oncoming car that blinded me skidded, bumped off the road and shot into the open field behind, before the driver stopped it. Two more flaring lights sped towards us and passed two feet away on the inside lane. A liquid stream of other headlights hurried in our direction, flashing madly at us.

The line of young poplars broke and I swung the Ferrari across the rough centre strip back to the right side of the Autoroute. At the same moment the Mercedes emerged from the other side of the poplar fence. I caught a glimpse of the incredulous, startled face of the driver as I swerved back in front of him.

His hands grabbed frantically at the wheel, pulling it to the right. The Mercedes careered out of control and went over the hard shoulder.

It plunged on and came to rest a hundred yards off the road with its nose in a deep drainage ditch. Its headlights went out suddenly and darkness swallowed it up.

'*Oh, Mon Dieu!*' moaned Madame Croissé and fainted. Jean-nine was wedged and silent behind the seats. She breathed loudly in her fright.

I ran a hand across my cold, damp face but kept the car going about eighty-five. It seemed like walking pace. But there was no question of stopping until I had put some distance between me and the *débâcle* on the Autoroute behind.

The Dino would be wanted by the *gendarmes* now, after its flagrant breach of lane discipline.

Twenty

After half an hour more of fast driving through the vineyards of Burgundy, blue and white knife-and-fork signs began appearing at the roadside. They promised a restaurant soon. The grape vines were not visible from the Autoroute, so I couldn't confirm immediately what I'd read – that they had suffered from bad weather and 1972 wasn't going to be a very good year. One thing I could confirm: it certainly hadn't been a very good year for my driving in Bourgogne.

The neon-lit, Formica-surfaced food dispensary of Jacques Borel appeared ahead. The restaurants, snack bars, shops, lavatories and other conveniences are built over and around the road like a gaudy bridge. The bright lights are very welcome to the stiff-legged, tension-weary motorway driver.

They were welcome to me for another reason.

I pulled quickly into the car park and sneaked the Dino into the darkest corner. It was as far as it was going. This trip at least.

Madame Croissé still sagged in her seat belt. I had ordered Jeannine to get out the bottle of Hine from the rucksack on which she was lying immediately after the trauma of my lane swopping. She had made her bemused mother drink straight from the bottle. Gradually she'd returned to something like full consciousness.

I jumped out to look at the buckled front of the Dino. The elegant handiwork of Pinin Farina was dented, mauled and scratched. The front of the car wore a crumpled, resigned expression as if it knew we had to go on without it.

After the chaos I had caused forty miles back I knew it wouldn't be long before the *gendarmes* were putting up roadblocks to welcome it.

The next car but three in the line was a white Citroën DS and it was the first one in which I found a door open. There was a vacuum flask on the back window shelf. I pressed this quickly into Jeannine's hand with ten francs and told her to run into the empty Quick Café to have it filled with black coffee.

As she dashed off I found myself hoping that Vadim hadn't stopped at Jacques Borel's for a snack at this moment. If he had, I should never see her again.

Although the owner of the Citroën had obligingly left a rear door open he hadn't left the key in the ignition. I raised the bonnet and found the wire running to the coil. It was just long enough. I sheared through the doubled-over end of it at the loom with the small penknife on my key-ring, bared it and connected it to the live pole of the battery. Then I started the engine.

I glanced quickly round, but nobody was running out from the restaurant to stop me. I hustled Madame Croissé into the back of the car and dumped my rucksack in beside her. I closed the bonnet and slipped behind the wheel as Jeannine dashed back with the flask of coffee. I looked under the column, prepared to try and break the steering lock. But I was in luck. It was an early DS20 and didn't have one. I was moving before Jeannine had closed the door.

We had been four minutes in the car park. I hoped the owners of the Citroën would linger over their meal to give us a good start. The first thing to do was to get off the Autoroute as soon as possible. The next turning to the left that came up was the N78 to Autun and I took it.

'Oh, the bruises on my 'ips!' Jeannine was pouting and rubbing herself on the passenger seat beside me. 'But eet ees such a relief to sit on a proper chair,' she said ruefully.

Madame, her mother, was stretched out on the rear seat, muttering distractedly to herself.

'I weel show you my bruises,' said Jeannine in a conspiratorial whisper, 'when we get to Jersey. Ooohh!'

I leaned over and pulled the vacuum flask from the glove compartment.

'Give your mother some of this,' I said gently. 'Try to forget your bruises for a bit. Perhaps I *will* look at them later.'

She did as she was told, after giving me the benefit of a sidelong smile of film-set wickedness.

Then she laced a steaming plastic cup of coffee for me with Hine and I gulped it down as I drove. After that I settled down to concentrate on the winding N78.

Here the wine of Burgundy was visible in the headlights at the unfenced roadside, hanging in black bunches at the bottom of the short, gnarled vines.

I tried to empty my mind of everything except driving quickly and safely out of the area and on to St Malo in time for breakfast. As soon as the owners finished their meal the *gendarmes* would be watching for the Citroën too.

I yawned an enormous, unstoppable yawn and looked at my watch. It was 2.30 a.m., Sunday morning.

Twenty-one

About six hours later through bleary eyes I saw a sign that said 'Restaurant avec Chambres' and pulled in to park. We were in the small village of Trans just below Mont St Michel. The hydrofoil and St Malo were only half an hour away.

Madame Croissé and her daughter had slept, twisted and grey-faced in their seats as the slate-coloured dawn came up.

I had a tired, dissipated feeling of having driven for too long and too far, without sleep. I had almost developed a squint watching for *gendarmes* to step out from the roadside, waving torches or East Germans to pop their heads out of cars, pointing guns. My mouth was sour, my eyes arched and there was a dull throbbing around my temples. I was as stiff as a starched poker. Apart from that I felt fine.

We stopped outside a café-restaurant called La Croix Verte where a woman was swabbing down the pavement with a bucket and mop. I wound down my window and asked if she could give me *petit déjeuner*.

'*Bien sûr, Monsieur*,' she said and smiled a broad, homely smile that could only have come from a good, simple person living a good, simple life.

At that moment she and her restaurant became the flame and I the moth, whatever else was happening in the ugly, uncaring world.

I got out and opened the passenger door.

'For your wife and daughter, too?' she asked, laying aside the mop and untying her apron. And smiling again.

I nodded dumbly. Madame Croissé and Jeannine were emerging slowly from the car, too befuddled with sleep and exhaustion to notice our new relationship. I had clearly grown old in the night.

The middle-aged angel of La Croix Verte set off to the back door of the nearby *épicerie* to procure croissants and bread for us. I deposited the Croissés inside, raised the Citroën's bonnet and disconnected the wire from the battery to stop the engine. Then I walked along the one and only street of sleepy, early-morning Trans to stretch my legs.

The sun was beginning to tussle with the slate-coloured sky over what kind of day it should be.

I stopped at the village war memorial. Sixty names of sons of the village who had died in the Great War were hewn into the stone. That must have practically decimated one-street Trans. The memorial had been used again, on the reverse side, for the Second World War. Only twelve names for that. An improvement of some kind for the village. There was no more room left on the plinth for the Third, I was thinking, when the billboard for that morning's newspaper outside a café opposite caught my eye.

'*Mort Sur Le Pont d'Avignon!*' shouted the bill from behind its trellis-work of thin wire.

My weary brain wouldn't accept that at first. Could it be I who was murdered? Had the drive through the night been a nightmare in limbo? Was I now teetering at Trans awaiting a final decision? Heaven or Hell?

I crossed the road to the café quickly. Inside, a group of men were sitting around drinking *pastis* from little thin-stemmed glasses, despite the early hour. A pile of papers, with '*La Nouvelle Republique du Centre-Ouest*' on the masthead in red, lay on a chair. The string round them had just been cut. I put down fifty centimes and raised my eyebrows at the *patron* as I reached out my hand. He grunted approval. Nobody else looked round. I walked back up the street, reading the story as I went.

Then I stopped.

The unidentified man found dead in the chapel on the bridge had a bullet hole between his eyes, the story said. I had to read almost to the end of the story to learn that he had also been shot in the legs. There were no papers on the body to identify who he was or what nationality. His suit appeared to have been made in Eastern Europe, the story said. A passer-by was quoted as having thought he heard shots as the bells on the bridge struck nine. But he couldn't be sure.

Who had killed the unfortunate Hans? Had I?

Impossible. I had never seen his face. It was hidden by the stone aperture. Had one of the other two gone back to help, found it impossible – and put him beyond interrogation?

I found I was back at the Croix Verte. I stuffed the paper in my pocket and went in. I said nothing of the story to the Croissés who were warming their hands on soup-bowl-sized cups of *café au lait*.

I began to think that for a freelance journalist I was missing out on the writing of a lot of good stories.

I ate two buttered croissants and drank two bowls of milky coffee with lots of sugar. I was glad Madame Croissé didn't feel inclined to talk. She didn't want to draw attention to herself. Her half-century-old face looked like the wrath of God over Egypt after the trauma of the night and cramped, fitful sleep. She snapped whenever she spoke to her daughter. Jeannine's fresh young face and cat-like stretching clearly annoyed her, reminded her too forcibly that her own beauty had crumpled and wasted.

I paid and led the way back to the car.

Jeannine saw the paper in my pocket as I started the engine. 'What ees the news?' she asked sleepily.

'Another rumour story from Peking, that's all. They think Mao might be dead again – for the hundred and fourth time.

We drove in silence to St Malo. I parked the Citroën near the Casino so that it would not point to the hydrofoil and dragged the rucksack out. I made a mental apology to its owner, remembered to leave him his vacuum flask and set off along the Quai St Vincent, shepherding the Croissés towards the Gare Maritime. There was a moment of panic at the hydrofoil ticket window when the question of passports came up. But there was a photo booth nearby and I was able to get day passes for them.

With a start I realized I was preparing to return looking exactly like the wanted man the Jersey CID were seeking – if you discounted the two days' growth of blue chin. Lack of sleep was making me careless.

I deposited my two charges in the café adjoining the ticket office and headed for the lavatories to change back into Weeks's jeans and tee-shirt.

A man in a short tweed overcoat and matching trilby hat pushed open the swing doors to the booking hall as I approached them. For a moment we were face to face. He opened his mouth as though to speak. But I turned and hurried into the lavatories.

96

As I got out of my suit into the dirty gardening clothes I told myself the man had wanted to ask the way to the ticket desk. An Englishman who recognized another. I combed my hair forward over my ears and forehead until I looked like a pasty-faced, blue-chinned insomniac, Roman idiot. Then I recalled I'd left the Croissés alone in the café. I just remembered to put the gold-rimmed spectacles on before I dashed out, dragging the rusksack. To my relief I could see their heads bobbing in desultory conversation through the glass partition of the café.

Then I stopped.

The man in the tweed coat and trilby was staring in my direction. He was standing just inside the swing doors, holding one leather glove in an already gloved hand. The other hand was in his coat pocket. Very English bearing. But the pocket in which he had his hand looked lumpy.

I cut across the hall well to his left and slipped into the café. The eyes under the brim of the tweed trilby followed me. I put the rucksack down on a chair beside Jeannine and Madame Croissé. They looked up at me curiously.

'You both ready for your sea trip?' I said with forced brightness, before they could speak. 'The Condor leaves in thirty minutes at nine thirty.'

'All I want to do, Monsieur Robson, is sleep and be safe,' said Madame. She had a resigned, dreary expression as if nothing else could touch her, as if she was beyond feeling after the events of the night.

Jeannine stared at my disgusting get-up in disbelief. 'What are you doing?' she asked incredulously. 'Are you a queek-change artist?'

I winked at her amorously, as I imagined Vadim might have done. 'I'll explain later,' I said. 'I've got something I must do now. If I'm not back by boarding time, get on without me. Take the rucksack, and ring the Kerensky farmhouse at the Jersey dock.'

Then I walked back towards the man in the tweed trilby.

Twenty-two

'Can I lend you a cloak and dagger to go with that outfit, Robson?'

The well-moulded English was perfect. I guessed it had taken the man in the tweed trilby about forty-five years of practice to perfect it – by way of an English public school, Oxford, the Brigade of Guards and the Foreign Office.

'Beg pardon, Guv,' I said, hunching my shoulders and shoving my hands into the pockets of the jeans. 'I didn't quite catch what yer just said, like.'

Pale blue eyes stared at me for a moment from under the brim of the tweed trilby. They were out of keeping with the rest of the face that was pulled into downward lines by years of expressing polite, urbane contempt for the fools around it. That expression was there now. But the clear, almost pretty, blue eyes looked as if they had been rented from another face.

'I think we might take a walk along the dock, Robson.'

He turned and went out through the swing doors without waiting for my reply, or to see if I was following.

I hurried obediently after him.

'Perhaps you'd be kind enough to tell me who you are, sir,' I said with exaggerated deference. I had dropped the flattened vowels of the East End.

I fell into step beside him going north along the Quai St Louis. He didn't reply but stared past me at the ships and cranes standing idle at the wharf in the quiet of Sunday morning.

'I'll call you Carruthers, then,' I said, cocking my head and looking sideways at him through half-closed eyes. 'Yes, you look like a "Carruthers" to me. Carruthers, from the British Embassy, Paris.'

He looked sharply at me without slowing his stride. The blue eyes narrowed. But he said nothing.

I looked down at his highly-polished toe-caps, the razor-line creases in the tweed trousers, the Moss Bros shorty coat and the button-up gloves. Then I looked at my own scuffed shoes, the muddied jeans, the tee-shirt. I sniffed loudly; I suspected I looked thoroughly ridiculous.

'You look thoroughly ridiculous, Robson,' he said, confirming my worst fears.

He was walking close to the edge of the dock now and I had to step over hawsers and bollards to keep up with him. He didn't seem concerned that he was leaving me so little room between him and the wooden piles of the wharf.

'You not only look thoroughly ridiculous, Robson,' he continued, 'but you've caused a lot of damned trouble. Not least getting me out of bed at five o'clock on Sunday morning to drive here from Paris.'

'Carruthers, I'm really sorry,' I said plaintively. 'Especially about getting you out of bed.'

He stopped suddenly and turned to face me. I stood with my back to a gap between two ships. Wavelets slapped noisily against the wooden piles twelve feet below. For several moments he just stared into my face without speaking.

'Carruthers?' I said interrogatively, raising my eyebrows and waiting attentively for him to speak.

His words were thin and flattened when they came out through his teeth, as if they had been maltreated during their confinement.

'Have you seen this?' He thrust a morning paper under my nose with the '*Mort Sur Le Pont d'Avignon*' headline.

'Yes,' I said, 'I have seen it. Nasty business by the looks of things.'

'We were watching the house, Robson. We had been watching it since Friday night.'

'Really,' I said.

'And you barged in from the blue and practically ruined the whole thing.'

'What do you mean "the whole thing"?'

'They killed their man on the bridge; I suppose you know that?'

'Well, I knew I hadn't,' I said, widening my eyes innocently.

'Fortunately for you, Robson,' said Carruthers, still hissing his maltreated words at me through thin lips, 'we managed to pick up the other two. Schwarz was found unconscious on the stairs. And his friend we picked up outside the café just after you drove off in the Ferrari like a doped-up teenager.' He paused for breath. 'It was he who had returned to the bridge to help the man presumably shot by you. Then he finished him off when he couldn't help. We found two kinds of bullet in him.'

'Look, Carruthers,' I said shortly, 'I don't take kindly to being lectured. I especially don't take to being lectured by well-dressed, psychotic strangers on the dockside at St Malo on blustery, autumn Sunday mornings.'

His look of contempt turned to a scowl.

'Perhaps you'd better make yourself clearer,' I said.

He took a deep breath. His eyes hadn't left my face since we stopped walking. 'Robson, you may look like a fool, dress like one and speak in funny accents.' His voice was so low I could hardly hear him. 'But one assumes there is a grain of sense somewhere inside your head.'

'One assumes it,' I said. 'Not without risk, mark you. But one may assume it.'

'I was called from London at 4.45 a.m. this morning and told to get up here to stop you, Robson.'

'I've already apologized about the early call. It *was* to the British Embassy, was it?'

'It *was* to the British Embassy,' Carruthers agreed heavily. 'Your instructions, Robson, were to go to Jersey. And stay there. Not to launch yourself on Avignon using your amateur dramatics flair for disguises and funny voices . . .'

'Just a moment,' I interrupted. 'What instructions? I had no instructions.'

'Your instructions from Smythe were to go to Jersey . . .'

'*Instructions* from Smythe?' I cut in. 'What do you mean *instructions* from Smythe? I had a personal telegram asking me, as a friend, to go and see him, that's all. Nothing else.'

Carruthers paused and considered his words carefully. 'London thought that was the best way to do it to begin with.'

He stood and rocked back on his heels giving little nods of his head without saying anything. As if he agreed that London had been *right* to think that was the best way to do it to begin with. I felt my anger rising.

'It was unfortunate that he died before he could tell you more,' said Carruthers with a shrug. 'We did it that way so the Kerenskys wouldn't suspect.'

I suddenly found the polished, self-possessed manner of the man in front of me intolerable. 'You smug bastard,' I spat the words out. 'You didn't know Smythe, I suppose . . .'

'No, I didn't. Awfully nice chap, so they say.' He continued to rock on his heels, holding the glove he wasn't wearing behind his back with both hands. 'You really shouldn't be so offended, Robson, at being kept just a tiny bit in the dark,' he said smoothly as I glared at him. 'You've worked for us enough on these foreign assignments of yours to know better. They sent me a summary of your dossier on the teleprinter at the embassy before I left. Don't pretend you don't know how we and you have to work – and why.'

He took out a yellow tin of State Express cigarettes, inserted one in a black and silver cigarette holder and lit it with a gas lighter from his overcoat pocket. The jet flame from the lighter resisted the gusting wind efficiently. I noticed that the bulky contents of the other pocket still caused a lump in the line of his coat.

I looked at my watch. It was ten past nine. I looked back towards the Gare Maritime. A few people were still arriving for the hydrofoil to Jersey and Guernsey. I hoped the Croissés were still waiting in the café.

'I've booked you on the eleven o'clock flight to London from Paris, Orly,' he was saying. 'My car's over there. Shall we go.'

The last three words were not a question.

'I want to go back to Jersey with the Croissés,' I said, feigning petulance.

'No, I don't think so,' said Carruthers in a matter-of-fact tone. 'London really would like you back. They want to talk to you.'

'Then they can talk to me after I get back from Jersey,' I replied, stamping my foot.

'They'd rather like to do it before you're arrested by the Jersey CID – or the French *gendarmerie*,' he said drily. 'You don't need to worry about Hartmann and his friend,' he added. 'They left the island rather hurriedly late last night. After the news of your visit to Avignon reached them, I expect. London are going to be very annoyed with you about that.'

I suddenly felt the weight of twenty-nine hours without sleep. What Carruthers had just said reached through to my thinking brain only very slowly.

'Why the hell should they be annoyed?'

'Look, Robson,' he said blandly. 'You seem to be particularly slow on the uptake this morning. I can't think why London ever allowed you to be involved in the first place. But if it will help you to make up your mind to come quietly to Orly with me, I'll explain what London will no doubt tell you later today.'

He spoke his words quickly, leaning towards me.

'Smythe worked for the East Germans as well as for us, London allowed him to be recruited by them in Berlin. We have people like Smythe in all the tax havens, to keep a finger on the pulse. He was told to dangle the bait of the Kerensky Trust in front of Hartmann's nose – and it was snapped up.'

'I don't get the reason why . . .' I began to interrupt.

'I'm coming to that, Robson, if you'll wait a moment, Carruthers said irritably. 'We know the Ruusian KGB and the other East Europeans are planning some pretty big operation – but we don't know what it is. You remember a hundred and five Russian diplomats were booted out of London not so long ago?'

Carruthers paused and ejected the stub of the State Express from the holder with its little spring action. He stuck the empty holder back in his mouth before continuing. 'They got ten million pounds in a forged contracts and invoices swindle in the Bahamas three months ago. Hartmann was involved in that. We have detected rumbling in other places, too – Liechtenstein, Hong Kong – which might be the beginnings of other attempted Communist money coups. Whatever the operation is, they obviously require a lot of Western currency to carry it through. And the tax havens they have rightly decided are well-stocked waters in which to fish.'

'Has anybody any idea why . . .' I started to ask again.

'There are plenty of theories, Robson,' he said testily: 'Big espionage drive against China from Hong Kong; intensive campaign in America to check exactly what defences we've got against the new Russian Fractional Orbital Bombardment

System; a new drive on Western party membership ... There are plenty of theories. But we don't know.'

'Might it not be a straight financial offensive?' I said. 'To heat up the world monetary crisis?'

'How would they do that, Robson?' he asked sarcastically. 'Have you suddenly become a financial wizard without telling us? One of the unsung Gnomes of Bradford?'

'Not exactly,' I said, 'but clearly it takes a mind trained as a junior reporter on the *Argus* to think it through properly. If they started moving large sums of money back and forth across national frontiers they could jeopardize the exchange rates and escalate the dollar crisis. A nice wrecking action with perhaps an international trade war among the capitalist countries to follow. It's just a thought which I offer you.'

Carruthers eyed me coldly. 'Whatever they're after, the trap was set to close so that we could find out. Then you started blundering around out of control.'

'But you've got what you wanted,' I put in slowly. 'Two East Germans held in Avignon. For questioning.'

'It should have been five – including Hartmann – not two,' he said softly. 'They may not know anything. Hartmann has slipped the net with the other one in Jersey. If we get nothing out of the Avignon pair you might be in bigger trouble than you are now.'

'How do you know Hartmann's gone?'

'A boat has been reported missing from Gorey. Hartmann and Co. seem to have got away to Carteret. It's only thirteen miles from Jersey to the Cherbourg peninsula at that point. The French SDECE may pick them up. But there's an evens chance they won't. We had two men in Jersey. They followed Hartmann to the meeting in the bunker with you. Kept out of sight of course. Now they've come to France to help the French look for them.'

Carruthers stopped talking and put his cigarette holder back in his pocket.

'What about the Kerenskys?' I asked. 'Nobody seems to have thought of them. They've been having a pretty rough time on your behalf.'

'I expect they'll survive,' said Carruthers. 'They've managed to before.'

I said nothing.

'Oh, and another thing,' he said, turning to walk towards the car park, 'London won't congratulate you on putting our Lyon man off the Autoroute earlier this morning either. Come on!'

I walked beside him.

It's funny you know, Carruthers, but before I met you I thought I'd done rather well in France,' I shook my head from side to side. 'I thought I'd had a lot of luck in France.'

Carruthers didn't reply. I noticed he had put his ungloved hand back in the lumpy pocket of the coat.

'So that white Mercedes 350 SLC wasn't the East Germans at all,' I said, musing out loud. 'I suppose if he'd managed to jolly well stop me they wouldn't have had to get you out of bed at four thirty, would they?'

Again Carruthers didn't reply. He just kept walking towards his car, as if the memory of the rude awakening still hurt him. I got the impression he was disgusted with me, too, for splitting an infinitive.

'I think I'll just run and get my rucksack,' I said.

We were at his car now.

'I'd leave it, Robson, if I were you.' His tone was patient, paternal. And his hand and what he had in it was making a nasty poke inside his coat pocket – in my direction.

I shrugged, walked towards the door he held open and hit him hard in the abdomen from close in. As he buckled forward I brought my knee up hard in his groin. I heard him grunt. I hit him low a second time.

He was leaning hunched against the side of the car as I ran back towards the Gare Maritime.

Twenty-three

The passengers for the Condor hydrofoil were just filing through the departure hall of the Gare Maritime when I got there. Men in drab suits were inspecting passports. Madame Croissé and her daughter were at the end of the line, looking anxiously over their shoulders.

I walked up and took the rucksack from Jeannine.

'Are you all right?' she said, staring up into my face. 'You are out of breath. Yes?'

'Yes,' I said. 'I just met somebody who thought he knew me. He's got a bit of stomach trouble. I saw him to his car.'

The passport inspector tore a piece off my pink card. I took a quick look round but there was no sign of Carruthers. We got into the bus to be taken up to the pier to the *hydroglisseur*.

On board Jeannine manoeuvred herself next to me. The airline-style seats were set in long rows and I sat at the end nearest the aisle. While her mother sank back and closed her eyes, she wriggled in her seat and looked naughtily at me from under her long, dark lashes. Now the tension was off the full frontal assault of her sex appeal was on again.

When the hydrofoil began to sway as it got up on its foils outside the harbour, she pretended that its motion was throwing her over towards my seat. Only the wool of her black sweater came between us as the craft rolled and she pressed the full, rounded softness of her breast surreptitiously against my bare arm.

The white hydrofoil swung on over the choppy sea. The slow, sustained rocking motion shook down my eyelids. They fell slowly and reluctantly, like a safety curtain in a theatre interval.

I opened my eyes again to see Jeannine bending forward to pick up my glasses from the floor. The sweat was cold on my forehead. I sat up.

'You were muttering and tossing in your seat,' she said, staring at me.

'I was dreaming . . . um . . . dreaming about you,' I said, with a flash of inspiration.

A delighted smile spread over her starlet's face. 'Was it in colour?' she asked eagerly. 'How did I look?'

At Jersey we disembarked and I gave the immigration officer the last pink piece of Frank Smith with his disreputable photograph on it. The same officer was on duty who had checked him out to France twenty-four hours earlier. He gave Frank the same look of disgust again – but he found no professional fault with him.

We took a taxi to the Kerensky farmhouse.

Inside the courtyard with the tall, white gates safely closed, emotional reunions took place. Joseph Croissé looked immensely relieved, sheepish, thankful, then sheepish again. None of which suited the shifty, ferret-faced little man.

He continued to embrace his wife and daughter tearfully. Madame Croissé had found enough energy to begin describing her ordeal in detail from the start as her husband led her towards the front door. George Kerensky smiled a broader smile than I had ever seen from him before and took her other arm. Jeannine and Rodica embraced. Then Jeannine turned and looked at me.

"E was *fantastique*,' she said, pouting and smiling at the same time.

'Welcome home, Errol Flynn,' Rodica said. She smiled, too, and put her arm around Jeannine's shoulders, still looking at me. 'You know that dates you.'

'What does?' I asked.

'Talking about Errol Flynn.'

'He *was* my hero, you know,' I said plaintively. 'Well,' I conceded, 'perhaps my father's. But I can't get to feel the same about your Che Guevaras, your Steve McQueens.' Then I thought of something. 'Jeannine thinks I look like Roger Vadim,' I said brightly.

'That still dates you,' said Rodica. She swung neatly on a finishing-school heel and walked Jeannine towards the house.

I was standing practising looking crestfallen when I saw Weeks in the shrubbery on the far side of the lawn. I went over and thanked him for the loan of his clothes – and put another request to him.

'I'll do my best, sir,' he said. 'But I can't promise. Nobody has ever asked me to get them before.'

Inside the hall George Kerensky came to me beaming. He gripped my hand and used exaggerated superlatives. 'You've done the trick,' he said jovially.

The London Sunday papers lay on a table in the hall. They, too, carried the '*Murder Sur Le Pont Avignon*' headlines. The sub-editors obviously liked that bit of French. Kerensky saw me looking at it and raised his eyebrows in an unspoken question.

'I'll tell you the details later,' I said. 'What I need now is a long sleep.'

'Yes, quite right, your eyes are red. You look as if you need sleep,' said Kerensky. 'But you've earned it. And now we can all sleep soundly.'

He patted me on the back.

'There's just one thing that's been worrying me,' I said. 'What about your brother in Switzerland?'

'He is coming tomorrow,' said Kerensky, still beaming. 'He will arrive at Jersey airport at ten o'clock. We take off at ten thirty.'

'Are you sure he is all right?'

'Of course, of course. I have spoken to him on the telephone yesterday and already again this morning. He assures me all is well.'

'Is he flying via London?' I asked.

'No, he is coming in his own plane.'

'Does he fly himself, then?'

'No, of course not,' said Kerensky, smiling broadly. 'If you had met Julius you would not ask that. He is — how shall we say? — delicate. Not a man of action.'

'Then he has his own pilot?'

'Yes, of course he has his own pilot,' said Kerensky. 'But why all these questions? Go and sleep. We will talk later.' He began to usher me along the hall towards the stairs.

'Just a minute,' I said. 'His pilot? Is he trustworthy? How long has he worked for your brother?'

'Trustworthy?' Kerensky was asking himself the question. 'I don't really know. I haven't met him yet. His last man was good. He brought him here several times. But now he has a new pilot. The other one left him recently.'

'How recently? When exactly?' I asked sharply.

'Oh, I think about two months ago . . . But I don't understand. Why all these questions . . .?' Kerensky was still smiling in the after-glow of the happy release.

'The new pilot,' I asked in a low voice, 'what nationality is he?'

'Swiss, I think,' said Kerensky, looking puzzled.

'German-speaking Swiss?'

Kerensky's face had become serious at last against its will. 'Yes,' he said, drawing the word out. 'He is German-speaking Swiss.' The implications of what he'd just said were dawning on him now.

'Why did your brother's last pilot leave him?'

Kerensky stared at me. 'We never really knew. He left suddenly without any explanation.'

A babble of voices came from the drawing-room. The three Croissés and Rodica were speaking rapid, excited French.

Kerensky continued to stare at me in silence. When he spoke again the old anxiety was back in his voice. 'You don't think . . .' his words trailed away.

'I don't know,' I said. 'Right now I need about twelve hours' sleep. We'll discuss it when I wake up.' I turned again towards the stairs. 'Meanwhile,' I said over my shoulder, 'try to phone your brother and tell him to do his utmost to come alone by a public airline. But it may already be too late.'

A minute later I was in the bedroom. Three minutes later I was asleep.

Twenty-four

'What do you think they will do?'

Kerensky's face was that of the gaunt, agitated vulture again as he asked me the question. He was seated in a green leather wing chair before the log fire. He sipped a brandy nervously. The brief elation I had seen on his face when I returned from St Malo served only to emphasize the haggard lines of anxiety that had returned now.

He had been unable to get any reply from his brother Julius in Switzerland.

The Hohenzollern clock chimed nine times. We were alone. I was feeling refreshed by ten hours of sleep. The Croissés, finally exhausted by their reunion, had apparently retired to bed in the late afternoon. The Portuguese staff were having a night off at the cinema in St Helier and Rodica was in the kitchen preparing dinner.

'My guess,' I said, 'is that Julius will arrive in his private plane tomorrow accompanied by his "Swiss" pilot – and maybe one or two other German-speaking companions. I would guess that Julius's blond-haired, pilot boyfriend was planted on him eight weeks ago as a backstop to the Avignon end of the operation.'

Kerensky had just explained why Julius had never married – in unambiguous terms.

'Now that the pressure on you through Avignon has been removed I would expect the thumbscrew to be applied through Julius,' I said.

I had described my trip to Avignon, missing out the conversation with Carruthers at St Malo. I left Kerensky with my original assumption that we had been chased on the Autoroute by a back-up group of East Germans. I said nothing of Clarence Smythe's role or how the Trust had been used as a sitting duck to decoy the Germans.

'Hartmann and his henchmen may have withdrawn from Jersey rather hurriedly for their own safety after the collapse of the Avignon defence,' I said, presenting Carruther's information as my own guesswork. 'But don't be surprised if they turn up tomorrow as passengers in your brother's private plane.'

I wondered if Hartmann might now be sitting in some draughty cell in Normandy. But I doubted whether the French would have picked him up. Even if they had, it wasn't the sort of thing that would be announced on the nine o'clock news.

'I think you had better give me more details about your Trust, how it works and what will happen at the flying meeting tomorrow,' I said. 'We might be able to anticipate Hartmann's moves then – and have a better chance of forestalling them.'

Kerensky moved abstractedly like a man living through an unending nightmare. He lit one of his short Dutch cigars without any sign of relish. 'Do you know anything about Trusts?' he asked through the haze of blue smoke.

'Treat me like an innocent child,' I said.

'Basically, putting your money into a trust means you give it all away. Perhaps the best-known kinds of trust are those set up by people with money for the benefit of their families. They seek to avoid crippling taxation in the form of death duties. So that their families may go on enjoying the family fortune instead of the government.'

'Doesn't that usually mean in England that the Trust must be set up at least seven years before the death of the man settling the money?' I put in.

Kerensky nodded. 'Yes, seven years before the death of the settler. You're not quite such an innocent child on the subject as you make out, Mr Robson. If he dies before seven years estate duty still has to be paid.'

He paused, deep in thought. The room was silent except for the crackle of the burning logs. The clink and clatter of Rodica's preparations came faintly from the kitchen.

'My father,' Kerensky went on, 'set up our Trust twelve years ago. He died seven years and three months later. He was a very determined man.' The smile of reminiscence on his emaciated face carried the warmth of affection. 'There are two different basic kinds of Trust, Discretionary Settlements and Non-Discretionary Settlements – with capital letters . . .'

He stopped as the door opened and Jeannine minced in.

'Jonathan,' she said, pouting, 'I'm awake now. Are you coming to look at zose bruises you gave me in ze night?'

She wore a long dress that she'd probably borrowed from Rodica. Her dark hair was brushed loosely down over her shoulders. She reached up her right hand to hold her hair back from her face and stood posturing, her left hip jutted exaggeratedly sideways so that the dress was drawn tight over its rounded curve. Her left wrist was held languidly against her waist. She'd probably read somewhere that seductive women looked at men in novels with 'smouldering' eyes. And she was trying to make hers smoulder as she looked at me.

Rodica appeared in the doorway behind her holding a Cordon Bleu cookery book. She had a smudge of flour on her nose. 'Jeannine, I wonder if you would like to lend me a hand in the kitchen,' she said, arching an eyebrow.

Kerensky smiled a thin smile of thanks at his daughter. She leaned forward to close the door as Jeannine wiggled out, pouting.

Rodica's eyes caught mine. She paused, then said, 'Jonathan, by the way, means "gift from Jehovah" in Hebrew. A looser translation for Jeannine's benefit might be "answer to a maiden's prayer", don't you think?'

The door swung shut and eclipsed the start of a smile.

'. . . Ours is a Discretionary Settlement,' Kerensky continued, ignoring the interruption. 'My father named his three sons as sole trustees with unrestricted powers of investment. Most trusts have a trust corporation like a bank or a firm of solicitors or accountants as trustees. But anybody can be a trustee. The main stipulation in our case is that we must meet once in twelve months in the presence of a legal representative acceptable to all three members.'

'Trust settlements sound to me if they're fairly pliable instruments,' I said; 'you seem to be able to stretch them which way you like.'

He nodded. 'True. A trust settlement is one of the loosest forms of legal contract.'

He drew on his cigar, drank some brandy and continued, 'Clarence Smythe usually came on the flight with us.' He paused again. 'Most trusts name a charity in their final clauses so that if all the beneficiaries are killed the money shall not be left ownerless.'

'What do you actually do at the meetings?'

'We approve the accounts and sign a joint letter to bankers in Switzerland saying that we have met. Then the Trust monies continue to reside in our names. We all have various holding companies and investment policy is decided on for a further year. But it's largely a formality. Smythe's firm was entrusted by my father with the task of affirming the once-yearly meeting. If the legal representative is not invited to attend the meeting by 3 October he has a standard letter which he sends to the Trust's main bank in Switzerland. This instructs that the entire amount of the fund be donated to named charities.'

Rain pattered against the window, driven by a rising wind. I got up and gave myself another drink. 'Wouldn't it look rather fishy if the RSPCA suddenly received an anonymous gift of twenty-five million?' I asked. 'If you'll pardon the pun.'

'The charities are numerous and dispersed so that undue

attention would not be attracted by enormous sums suddenly appearing from nowhere,' Kerensky said. 'The letter confirming our meeting must arrive at the Swiss bank by 5 October annually. This letter has to be countersigned by the legal representative. Thus the standard letter from his office about the charities is countermanded.'

'But what does the term "Discretionary" mean?' I asked.

'It means that we wish, as long as we are unanimously agreed. You have probably guessed that the Trust was set up by my father in this form because of . . .' he paused to find the right words, '. . . because of certain frictions between members of the family. We are not a united family, Mr Robson, in the normal sense.' He smiled a grim smile. 'We are only united by our fortune.'

'Together we stand – with money. Divided we fall – broke,' I said.

'Exactly. We channel our monies from the Trust to our family holding companies. I have one registered in the Bahamas. Virtually no taxes are payable there. No balance sheets are requested, no profit and loss accounts. My brothers have similar companies.' He stopped as if suddenly regretting the extent of his confidences to a virtual stranger. But he continued after a moment. 'I, of course, control other orthodox interests which I declare to the tax authorities and pay normal taxes on them.' Kerensky looked up at me. 'Don't pull a long moral face, Mr Robson.'

'A tax dodger is a tax dodger, in my view, wherever he lives,' I said.

Kerensky grunted. When he spoke again the guttural rasp I had noticed on the phone the first time was back. 'There is a clear difference between tax avoidance and tax evasion, Mr Robson,' he said. 'Evasion is the easiest thing in the world to do. You simply make a false declaration; you break the law. Tax avoidance means doing everything permissible within the tax laws to minimize your liability.'

'But the tax havens,' I said, 'what the French so elegantly call *les paradis fiscaux*, operate only to the advantage of those who can afford to pay a high price to "avoid". They look to me like a kind of last-ditch defence by pure capitalism against increasingly socialized government. Millionaires are being squeezed like pips out of an orange from their mainland homes to the fiscal paradise islands.'

Kerensky relit his cigar which had gone out.

'There is a lot of emotional, moralistic indignation aroused by the tax havens,' he said, raising his head. 'But they exist because they do a job that suits both sides. If everybody earned the same amount of money there would be no problem in administering tax laws. But Western society admits of individual differences and tax havens, as I see it, are a very sophisticated expression and extension of this.'

'I think I shall call you "the New Right",' I said.

'I beg your pardon? You're not quoting psalms at me again, are you?'

'No, not this time. But to me this rush of money into the offshore islands in recent years smacks of the same kind of discontent with government expressed by banner-carrying students of the New Left – in their demonstrations. The New Right is protesting more subtly by moving its money quietly out of government's reach.'

I bent forward to throw another log on the red embers in the fireplace. It fizzed and the pungent aroma of burning resin mixed with the smoke. I dusted my hands together.

'It has been dimly perceived, hasn't it,' I asked, 'that the tax havens might be used for manipulating the world currency markets?'

'Yes, it is a danger,' said Kerensky. 'Speculators have much more freedom for manoeuvre.'

'But what perhaps hasn't been perceived *at all* is that the Communist half of the world could find a chink in the West's economic armour in the fiscal paradises. Surely they must already hold funds – in numbered accounts in Switzerland say – to finance their operations in the West. Now they obviously are trying to build up larger reserves of currency, fast. I think the attempt to grab your twenty-five million may be part of a larger operation to intensify the West's monetary crisis, to put the skids under the Western economies.'

Kerensky's eyes narrowed. 'Isn't that projecting things a bit too far, Mr Robson? They may just be short of hard cash.'

'Look,' I said, 'if the Communists got their hands on say a hundred millions or more, they could do a lot of damage in the world currency markets, swinging it around buying and selling currencies and even commodities erratically, couldn't they?'

'I suppose they could,' he said slowly. He put his fingertips together and stared at the ceiling. 'Yes, for example, the pound weakens considerably every year at the time of the American tobacco harvest. Sterling has to be used to buy dollars to pay for the tobacco. The same thing happens with the simple forward selling of other currencies. The deutschmark or the dollar or any currency could be attacked. God knows there've been enough exchange rate crises in the last few years. Currency markets tend to react emotionally, psychologically.'

'Maybe they have had a hand in what has happened already,' I said. 'Perhaps now they are tanking up their reserves for a bigger effort. The pound, the franc and the dollar have all been hit in the recent past by large, sudden movements of funds by speculators. What's to say who they are behind their holding company masks? Hartmann's political chiefs may be trying to stoke up the crisis again in the hope of another trade war or Wall Street crash. That would set the West on its economic ear. Unemployment, slumps, strikes. The creation of what Marxists refer to in hushed tones as "a revolutionary situation".'

I could tell by the way Kerensky turned his gaze from the flickering fire to stare at me that he had begun to see it as a possibility.

'Why did you put your Trust in an aeroplane instead of registering it in the normal way?' I asked. 'There would still be enormous tax advantages, wouldn't there?'

'There would,' said Kerensky. 'I suppose it boils down to this. We didn't wish to commit our money to the arbitrary control or interference of any one government, or any one body of law. A trust is usually registered where the trustees are resident or where it is signed. Ours was signed in the air outside territorial waters. You might see it as some kind of ultimate projection of free choice. We wished our money to be free, or as free as possible, wanted to row our own boat.'

'Why, incidentally, didn't you meet on a ship?' I asked.

'Because legally a ship is the territory of the country under whose flag it sails. A plane isn't. It's a flying no-man's-land.'

'You wanted to go one better than the tax havens really,' I said. 'And now you've brought on yourselves some very arbitrary interference indeed.'

Kerensky stared into the flames again and said nothing. As he spoke the butt of the cigar had burned short between his fingers without his noticing. He dropped it suddenly as the red glow reached his skin. At that moment he looked very frail and accident-prone.

'Which brings us back to Hartmann,' I said, 'and his efforts to hijack your own private goldmine in the sky. I think he will try to get aboard the plane and make you sign the entire amount of the Trust over to some bank account in Switzerland, or somewhere, where it will be at their disposal. These letters will be presented to your Swiss banks before the 5 October deadline. The Kerensky family will be twenty-five millions worse off and the disciples of Marx and Lenin will be a big step nearer to achieving their current objective, whatever it is.'

Kerensky sat and sucked his burned finger. Then he passed a hand slowly over his screwed-up face.

The door opened and Rodica called us into the dining-room for pheasant *Vallée d'Auge*.

Twenty-five

After dinner I went to the bedroom and took my battered portable typewriter from its case. For an hour I typed rapidly by the two-finger 'pick and peck' method, which is the way most Fleet Street reporters type their stories daily into the pages of the national press.

Dinner had been a meal of mixed moods. Kerensky tried to hide his apprehension – and probably succeeded with everybody except Rodica. I noticed her glance at him from time to time, concern crinkling the corners of her eyes. We had agreed that he should tell his brother Joseph of our suspicions about tomorrow's flight after dinner.

Madame Croissé and Jeannine were elated and refreshed, laughing and giggling at their lucky escape. At times they became jarring and a little hysterical. Rodica said she had spent the afternoon playing golf. But she was subdued and infected by her father's fear although he was trying to hide it.

I missed coffee and got away to the bedroom as soon as I could.

I was typing the last few lines and shuffling the pages of typescript into order when I heard the bedroom door open and close behind my back. I didn't turn round but went on picking and pecking. I felt two hands fall lightly on my shoulders either side of my neck.

I spoke without looking up from the typewriter. 'Jeannine,' I said patiently, 'it was very exciting when you twiddled your fingers in my hair in the car. And you made me quite breathless every time the hydrofoil rolled and threw you against me.' I paused and breathed deeply. 'And as for those bruises, well I'm sorry you got them rolling around in the car. But right now I am very busy. Perhaps later when I've finished . . .' I didn't get to the end of the sentence.

'Don't look now, but it's the cook,' said the voice above my head.

'The cook?' I said in an outraged voice. 'Good heavens, then the only person in this household who hasn't yet tried to seduce me is Fernando!'

I stopped typing, turned and looked up at Rodica. She was smiling. A small but genuine smile.

Then her face became serious again. 'If we can ignore your amorous adventures for a moment, Jonathan, I'd like to talk to you.'

She used my first name naturally and unselfconsciously. I liked that. At the same time she let her hands fall from my shoulders and stepped back to sit down in a chair beside the bedroom desk.

I was glad she did. I might have done something trite and sentimental otherwise. Thoughtless emotional reactions with

116

comparative strangers are rarely as polished as they are in film scripts.

'There's something wrong, isn't there?' She held her hands quietly in her lap but her expression was tight between the eyebrows.

I looked at her for a moment without speaking. Kerensky had not wanted to worry her with our new suspicions. 'How do you mean, something wrong . . . ?' I let the question hang.

'There's something else, something my father won't tell me about. Clearing up the mess in Avignon hasn't solved the problem, has it? I can tell from his face and his whole manner. I want you to tell me.'

She sat staring at her lap, waiting. She wore a purple woollen jersey with a plain grey skirt. Her purple wool stockings matched the sweater exactly. A large, flat Cross of Lorraine of dull, planished silver hung on a chain around her neck. The subdued lights of the bedroom shone dully on the copper hair that was pulled back severely from her face in a black ribbon and fell in a cascade behind her. She looked like a very beautiful nun.

She looked up again suddenly. 'And whether you tell me or not, I'm coming with you on the flight tomorrow.'

I opened my mouth to speak, but she hurried on.

'If there is danger for my father then I want to be with him.' She had an air of quiet, assured defiance. 'I *will* be there. But I would prefer you to tell me what it is that he is afraid of, *now*.'

'All right,' I said slowly. 'I think the East Germans might try to pull something else. I think they might have had a secret hold over Julius – maybe without him knowing – for some time. When he flies in tomorrow, the Kerensky Trust may be back where it started – with a gun at its head.'

She bit her lip. 'I thought it was something like that.'

I offered cigarettes and lit them.

'What will you do? Have you some plan?' she asked.

'No, not really. I suppose I shall rely again on . . .'

'. . . on-the-spot inspiration?' she said quickly.

'Well, yes. If anything.'

'Seeing Robson in action has obviously had great impact on Jeannine. I want to be there for that reason, too,' she said, looking at me with narrowed eyes through the smoke of her cigarette.

Then she suddenly smiled self-consciously. 'That thing the other night – my God it seems years ago – that really seems terrible now. I hope you don't think that I'm the kind of cheap . . .'

'I've forgotten it ever happened,' I said gently. 'I think I have some idea of how you and everybody else in your family is feeling . . .'

'But I suppose what I wanted to say,' she said looking away from me, round the room, then down at her lap, 'is that . . . well that I don't really think of you now as a bullet-headed thug, or whatever I said . . . And that . . . Oh for God's sake.' She broke off, embarrassed and angry with herself.

I smiled in the uncomfortable silence that followed. She looked at me and sucked in smoke fiercely. This made her cough and her eyes watered.

'Are you trying to say that secretly you were really beginning to enjoy yourself when I stopped you?'

She flushed angrily again. 'No I'm not! I've never tried to do anything like that before . . .'

'That, if I may say so, was obvious.'

'Don't be so damned patronizing,' she said quickly. 'I thought somebody with crude sensibilities would respond to crude methods.'

I laughed outright this time.

She glared at me again. But a smile was trying to find its way through. 'Perhaps you really *are* a bullet-headed thug,' she said at last. 'Maybe that's what's making me so incoherent.' She stood up, paced across the room, came back and stood looking down at me. 'I know my father has offered you a hundred and fifty thousand pounds,' she said, drawing hard on her cigarette. 'But that wouldn't be much use to a dead man. My aunt told me you took considerable risks in Avignon. I don't know what part of you makes you go on helping us. But whatever it is I wanted to thank you. The danger is really none of your business and I would think no less of you if you walked out and left us to it.'

I smiled inanely.

'I really don't know why you are going on with it. You were very hostile to us at first.' She sat down again.

I said nothing. I sat and wondered why, too. I suppose I thought a hundred and fifty thousand was worth the risk. But then there was Clarence Smythe, playing aces from his sleeve, Carruthers, rocking on his heels on the dock at St Malo, saying London thought it best to play it that way to begin with. There were the ever-recurring assignments in Vietnam, Bengal, Berlin, all points east – and west. An untidy, unsatisfactory life, messy, without much meaning. What was at forfeit really?

'Remember I told you there was no such thing as an unselfish act,' I said. I held my right elbow in my left palm and peered at the twisted yellow and orange strands of tobacco in the end of the cigarette. They were damp and the cigarette paper was moist from my mouth. 'I may have forgotten completely what happened the other night,' I said, 'in one sense. But maybe I've suddenly come to realize I like the scenery in this drama. That's maybe why I want to stay on stage and not hurry off into the safety of the wings.'

I stubbed out my cigarette then got to my feet to pace up and down. 'I may have forgotten it,' I said to the heavy curtain drawn across the window, 'but I might be happy to have my memory jogged some time.' I stopped talking. I sensed it was her turn to be smiling now behind my back. I swung round. 'But look. I think this idea of yours to come on the flight tomorrow is crazy.'

'Crazy or not,' she replied calmly, 'I'm coming. My father never refuses me anything if I really want it. Anyway I was personal assistant to a Madison Avenue advertising executive for two years. I think I can be very useful at crucial meetings.'

'Did the executive think so?' I asked.

'For a time at least. He married me.' Her voice gave no particular inflection to the announcement.

'What happened?'

'There seemed to be fewer crucial meetings when I was his wife than when I was his personal assistant. Crucial meetings went on – but I wasn't in them.' She dropped the finished cigarette into an ashtray. She didn't leave it alone until it was as dead as the subject she'd dropped with it.

119

She looked up suddenly. 'Were you ever married?' she asked quietly.

'I'm what's known in Fleet Street as a re-tread bachelor.'

'*Re-tread* bachelor?'

'Like the tyres of a car that have worn once and been resurfaced, you know?'

She started to smile.

'Don't smile,' I said. 'A re-tread looks as good as the new product – but in fact if used, it wears out in half the time. It's been through the mill; there's not so much mileage in it as there looks.'

I sat down again opposite her.

'Look,' I said at last, 'I think you ought to know I have to be out early in the morning. I've got to get to the airport first thing to persuade the pilot of the charter aircraft with an enormous bribe from your father. He has got to give up the aircraft into my doubtfully competent hands. And his uniform.'

'All right, I'll go and lock Jeannine up so you can get some sleep,' she said, getting up to go.

'If you're really set on coming perhaps you can look after something in the plane for me,' I said. 'Weeks, I hope, will get it by the morning. It will be a small cardboard box. I'll explain fully later.'

She walked towards the door. She half turned as if to say something, then thought better of it. She reached for the door handle.

'You look like a very beautiful nun,' I said smiling. She smiled back as she went out of the door.

An hour later the house was quiet. I had turned out the light and was lying on my back staring into the darkness. I saw the door open and close. I saw the silhouette briefly against the dimmed lights of the passage.

'Come in, Fernando,' I called. There was no reply for a moment.

'I've come to jog your memory.' The voice at my ear was a whisper.

I reached out. There was no immediate tempest or storm. The night outside was quiet.

'I admire you most of all because you're not frightened,' she said from the darkness close beside me.

'Frightened?'

'Of tomorrow.'

'You're quite wrong,' I whispered. 'I'm terrified.'

There was a long silence.

'I'm very frightened, too,' she said softly.

Twenty-six

I was sitting at the controls of the American-built Riley Executive 400 half an hour before we were due to take off. I had borrowed another pair of Kerensky's gold-rimmed spectacles – a pair I could see through this time without removing them. I pulled the blue and gold pilot's cap further down over my forehead as I peered at the instrument panel. If Hartmann did come I wanted to remain unrecognized for as long as possible.

The part of me that concerned itself with looking for good and bad omens had been ridiculously pleased at the sight of the Executive 400 outside the charter company's hangar.

If I'd been able to choose the plane in which to fly a party of warring millionaires and Communist agents around over the Atlantic, I'd have asked for a Hawker Siddeley Dove light transport. Not only because they've been making it since 1945 and it is tried and true. But also because I had done most of my professional piloting in Doves during a year flying over the bush helping a friend work up an African charter company.

Fate and the Kerenskys hadn't obliged me with a Dove – that was too much to ask. But the Riley was the next best thing, a modernized, re-engined and re-styled American conversion of that sturdy old crate. To make it fit for tired business moguls the Riley Aeronautics Corporation had given the Dove new power plants – two Lycoming 400 horsepower engines, a restyled cabin and little luxuries like an air-stair door.

I was sitting in the Riley Dove half an hour before take-off to give myself plenty of time for a careful pre-flight check. I'd kept my Instrument Rating up since Africa but hadn't logged much more than minimum hours at odd club weekends since then.

The pilot's dark blue uniform with its thin bars of gold braid wasn't a bad fit. I had put it on in the back office of the charter company. The pilot was roughly my size. He had looked reluctant at first. But he had finally overcome his reluctance at the sight of the two thousand pounds in five-pound notes Kerensky had given me to persuade him. I told him it was best not to try to reason why – and went to the tower to file the flight plan.

It was a simple VFR plan a hundred and fifty miles out due west of Jersey to where the warm waters of the Gulf Stream hit the cold currents of the English Channel – and back. It showed us returning with a southerly swing over Brest and the Brittany coast, then north-east home to Jersey. A two-hour flight – enough time for any well-conducted business meeting. I hoped it would be enough time for a badly conducted one, too.

The clear, clean morning was brilliant with sunlight and the sky was an uncompromising cobalt blue. The kind of day for which Visual Flight Rules were invented.

A blue and white BUABAC 1–11 from Gatwick arrived on the runway with a thump and ran on fast before reversing its engines with an earth-shaking roar. A red-winged Viscount taxied out, hauling more of BEA's passengers towards Heathrow. Little yellow ten-seater Islanders of Aurigny Air Services darted cheekily in and out among the lumbering airliners, shuttling handfuls of people around between the Channel Islands and France. Jersey Airport was working its way through one of its usual busy mornings.

I saw a Rolls come to a halt in the car park. George Kerensky, his brother Joseph and Rodica climbed out and walked over towards the Riley Dove. They were joined by another tall, thin man with a briefcase who emerged from his own car. I guessed this was a partner of Clarence Smythe's firm come to fulfil his role as legal observer – the way the Trust deed said he should.

Kerensky introduced me to him when they came on board. 'Just come to see fair play,' the solicitor said with a foolish smile.

'I hope you don't see any foul play,' I replied. He looked sharply at me as if he'd suddenly bitten on something sour.

Rodica was wearing the same purple sweater and the same colour stockings she'd worn last night. And the big silver cross. When she came up the steps there was no special affection in her greeting to me. Except perhaps her eyes held their smile a fraction longer than they might otherwise have done. She had left my room with as little fuss in the middle of the night.

Joseph Croissé looked smaller and more harassed than ever. His eyes flicked shiftily round the cabin before he seated himself in one of a set of four facing seats. He placed his black leather briefcase on the floor beside him. Both he and Kerensky wore black jackets and striped trousers. Correct attire, I supposed, for matters of high finance at three thousand feet.

'Rodica,' I said quietly, 'did Weeks give you anything?'

She nodded and came forward with a large, black briefcase. She opened it to show me. It contained a single box of strong cardboard about twelve inches long and six inches wide. Weeks had done as I'd asked and tied it with a single strand of string in an easy-to-release bow.

'What is it?' she asked, looking from the box to my face.

I closed the briefcase and handed it back to her. 'Keep it by your seat out of sight,' I said. 'If I want to use it I'll say, "Bring me my briefcase". But don't. Just open it and untie the string and take the lid off the box.'

'But what is it?' she asked again with a puzzled expression. 'A bomb of some kind?'

'If I told you, you might not want to fly with madcap Errol Flynn,' I said. 'Just think of it as the box for my collapsible, high-heeled sea boots. And sit here,' I said, pointing to the passenger seat nearest to the controls.

I looked at my watch. It was exactly ten thirty. There was still no sign of Julius's private plane. Kerensky stood in the open doorway, peering out at the runways with crinkled brows.

The airport buzzed with the coming and going of light aircraft. Occasionally the sound of their engines was overlaid by the roar of a jet, a Viscount or some heavy freighter. Behind the green glass of the control tower small head-and-shoulder figures directed the ceaseless flow of aircraft with no apparent effort.

123

The solicitor sat with his briefcase balanced primly on his knees, clearing his throat nervously. Nobody spoke. By ten thirty-five there was still no sign of Julius. Nevertheless I asked the tower for start-up clearance and ran the engines up. I did a practice take-off check just to reassure myself. All gauges were green. Still nobody was speaking in the cabin behind me. The solicitor was becoming apprehensive.

'Is there . . . ahem . . . is there anything wrong, may I ask, Mr Kerensky?' he said at last. He clearly hadn't known Clarence too well. And he hadn't thought to connect his death with the Kerensky Trust.

Kerensky still stared out of the door of the plane. He muttered something inaudible in reply without turning round. The solicitor clutched his briefcase and continued to clear his throat from time to time.

A few minutes later a new red and white Piper Seneca with Swiss registration letters dipped down towards the runway from the eastern end of the island.

We waited. The Riley Dove's twin engines idled. The solicitor still cleared his throat audibly against their subdued roar.

The Seneca rolled to a stop a hundred yards away after taxiing quickly and skilfully off the runway. For two minutes the door remained closed as if those inside were involved in a discussion.

Then it opened.

The first man down wore a long black coat with an Astrakhan collar and black Homburg hat. He clutched a document-case under his arm.

'That's not Julius,' said Kerensky, watching anxiously through the open door.

I wondered for a moment if it were a banking friend of Julius. Perhaps he had spent the weekend with him. Perhaps everything was all right. The man in the Homburg turned back towards the Seneca's doorway, holding a bowler hat and umbrella out towards the next man coming down.

'That's Julius,' Kerensky said.

I got quickly into the driving seat, put on the gold-rimmed glasses and kept my back squarely to the cabin. I looked sideways and saw Julius step down. His quick, mincing strides identified him immediately. He ignored the bowler hat and umbrella held out by the man in the Homburg and walked past him.

George Kerensky was waving to his brother from the doorway. The man in the Homburg hurried along behind Julius, still holding the bowler and umbrella towards his back as if in supplication. An athletic-looking man with yellow-blond hair was last out of the Seneca. He carried his pilot's cap in his hand and hurried after the other two.

When they were fifty yards away I realized that the man in the Homburg was squat, thick-set. And I saw that the bowler hat he held out in his right hand to his apparent superior was swivelling slightly as he walked, as though on a pivot.

The *pfennig* finally dropped.

The man in the Homburg was Hartmann and the hat in his right hand which he held towards Julius's back covered a gun.

I called the tower quickly and asked for taxi clearance.

'Yankee Tango, you're clear to taxi, runway two-seven. QNH one zero one five.' The voice of the controller was matter-of-fact. Yankee Tango or YT was the Riley Dove's call sign, the last two letters of its registration G-ATYT. I read back the clearance, set the altimeter and prepared to lift my feet from the brakes.

'Tell Julius to get up the steps fast,' I told Kerensky urgently under the cover of the engine noise. 'Then try to close the door behind him.'

The engines whined to a higher note and I raised my toes slightly on the brakes. Two white-overalled ground staff men looked across in alarm, seeing our door was still open.

'Quickly, Julius!' yelled Kerensky. 'Up the steps, fast!' He leaned out, ready to swing the door closed.

Julius paused to glance over his shoulder as he reached the bottom of the steps. That was his mistake. Hartmann reached forward with his left hand and grabbed Julius by the sleeve. Then in the same moment he appeared to prevent him from tripping and assist him smoothly up the steps into the plane.

I turned quickly to face forwards. I heard Hartmann enter the plane behind Julius. The blond pilot climbed the steps last and closed the door. He slammed the latch shut.

'All right, pilot,' said Hartmann in his strongly accented English. 'We are all here now; take it away.'

I eased my feet up from the brakes and rolled the Riley Dove out towards the holding point at the end of the runway, swallowing hard as I went.

Twenty-seven

'Yankee Tango, ready to take off when clear,' I told the tower through the little boom microphone which jutted in front of my mouth from the headset.

I ran the engines up to that roaring, whining pitch that precedes the surge forward along the runway. The Riley Dove shuddered and strained at its brakes.

The cabin had a small mirror mounted above the instrument panel like most single-pilot charter aircraft. It helps the pilot to check what his freight – human, animal, vegetable or mineral – is doing. As I finished my take-off check I glanced in it.

I saw Hartmann toss aside the bowler hat that had covered his right fist, revealing the squared-off shape of a Russian-made automatic pistol. He pointed it towards the three Kerensky brothers who were strapped in the facing seats. They stared at the gun transfixed.

I couldn't see Rodica in the mirror because she sat directly behind me.

'You're clear to take off, Yankee Tango. Runway two-seven, wind westerly light.' The impersonal tones of the controller showed him oblivious to the fact he was clearing an aircraft in which a Communist was holding a gun on three multimillionaires.

'Look here, what the devil is this?'

The solicitor, who was very concerned, had risen impulsively from his seat at the sight of the gun. His dignity was outraged and for a moment he showed a blind, thoughtless courage.

'Who are you?' demanded Hartmann in an ugly tone.

'I'm a solicitor.'

126

Without a word Hartmann brought the pistol down with a quick economic movement of his arm. The solicitor fell sideways on his seat, a gash on the side of his head brightening with blood. The noise of the racing engines drowned the thud of the blow and the cry of the solicitor. I saw the dumb mime of violence being enacted in the mirror, at the same moment that I released the brakes.

The Riley Dove threw itself forward along the runway and gathered speed. When the needle touched eighty knots I lifted her off. I climbed over the flat sands of the wide beach and headed out over St Ouen's Bay, lifting the landing gear. The nose of the plane pointed on a bearing straight out to Newfoundland. But that was two thousand miles away across the Atlantic. We were only going a hundred and fifty miles out and back.

Hartmann had scrambled into his seat when the momentum of take-off threw him off balance. As I climbed I looked into the mirror again and saw the solicitor, lying crumpled and unconscious. He wouldn't be seeing any more play for a few hours – fair or foul. I levelled out at three thousand feet and trimmed the controls, still heading due west.

I had got Fernando to give me a short back and sides with the kitchen scissors before I left for the airport. I hoped the glasses and the peaked cap pulled well down had changed my appearance sufficiently to prevent Hartmann recognizing me from the passenger seats. The headset and microphone boom I wore helped obscure my face.

The light wind was daubing splashes of cream on the face of the grey-green Channel below. The lush island of Jersey, richly endowed by nature and tax laws, fell away behind. It was the first time I'd taken a plane off and not been exhilarated by the clean, pure simplicity of life seen from a detached seat floating above it all. Perhaps that was how a flying, disembodied and gullible God had seen things in the beginning. It was the blond German coming forward to hold a black pistol against my temple that spoiled the sensation particularly for me this time.

Behind us Hartmann began to conduct a fast, efficient business meeting – waving his automatic like a conductor's baton.

127

'The annual meeting of the Kerensky Trust is open,' he declared in English. A small, virulent smile spread its tentacles around the corners of his mouth. 'We shall try to be brief. Who will read the accounts?'

He fanned the gun sideways in the white, staring faces of the Kerenskys. He stood hunched over them, a thick-set predator.

'Come on, gentlemen, the accounts.'

The blond man ignored what was happening behind him. He stood looking down at my hands on the controls and peering forward through the windscreen. He stood sideways on so that he could watch Rodica sitting behind me, too. I couldn't see her but guessed from her silence she was fighting to put a calm face on her fear. Then I heard her ask if she could tend the wound of the unconscious man, slumped on the seat behind her.

'Stay where you are,' said the blond man emphatically.

The Riley Dove droned on in the bright sky. I took another glance in the mirror and saw Julius reaching furtively down beside his seat.

The deep, black sockets of Hartmann's eyes swung on him. 'What are you doing?' he snapped.

'I have the accounts here; I was going to read them,' Julius croaked. His fear made his lisp even more pronounced.

He shuffled some papers from a slender black document case. He began to read details of international investments made in the names of different holding companies since November last year.

'Just the total,' Hartmann interrupted angrily. He moved the automatic to within an inch of Julius's chin. He gulped and rustled through the papers once more with shaking hands.

The paleness of George Kerensky's face had taken a yellow tinge. He stared ahead of him with a growing expression of desperation. I began to fear he would lose his head and provoke Hartmann to more violence. Joseph Croissé sat shifting his eyes around more wildly than ever before. Spasmodic twitches of fear contorted his narrow features.

'The total assets of the Trust as held in the numbered accounts in Zurich on October 1st . . .' Julius stopped and glanced up nervously at the gun in front of him. His eyes shifted to the blond

128

man beside me. They rested on his broad shoulders and blond hair for a moment, with a hurt, wounded expression.

'Come on, lover boy!' Hartmann knocked the automatic roughly against the side of Julius's bony jaw and motioned towards the papers.

'The assets of the Trust on October 1st stood at ... at ... twenty-five million, seven hundred and eighty-three thousand pounds,' Julius added hoarsely. Then he stopped and stared up at Hartmann.

'A very good result, if I may say so,' said Hartmann. He reached behind him with his free hand. He picked up his own document-case, unzipped it with his teeth and put it down on the seat. He reached inside and pulled out several sheets of paper.

'The next item on the agenda, gentlemen, is disposal of assets under the Discretionary Powers of the Trustees.' He put heavy, sarcastic emphasis on the words to convey the capitals. 'You will all sign this letter.' He waggled the gun in their faces again.

'It is very short and simple. All you have to do is insert the sum just mentioned by your brother Julius and sign your names. I'll read it to you,' Hartmann cleared his throat. He was enjoying himself. 'We the undersigned desire to dispose of ... insert the figures mentioned ... to the account of Hartmann Investments Ltd, at Liechtenstein in the bank mentioned below. This is our joint and unanimous will!'

He thrust the letter under the noses of each of the Kerenskys in turn. Then he put it down before George Kerensky.

The man who had survived Auschwitz hesitated for a long while, his pen held poised, his face working, his breathing fast and shallow.

Suddenly he looked up from the unsigned letter.

'I won't sign it, you foul bastard!'

He spat in Hartmann's face and stared defiantly at him. His aged and worn face quivered, but the firm set of his scrawny jaw revealed the iron will that had enabled him to survive the horrors of his imprisonment in Poland. Perhaps the memory of humiliations there strengthened him now.

'Shoot, damn you! I won't sign!'

His breath hissed through his nose. His mouth was clamped shut.

Hartmann was unmoved. Without blinking he took out a handkerchief and wiped his face. Then he turned and pointed his gun towards the seat behind me where Rodica sat.

The click of the safety catch being removed carried clearly inside the cabin above the steady drum of the twin engines. Kerensky's mouth fell open and his look of loathing changed to fear – not for himself but for his daughter.

'I'll count to five, Kerensky,' said Hartmann.

Rodica was silent. I cursed myself for letting her come – she made the perfect hostage. Hartmann couldn't shoot anybody else until he'd got his signatures.

Kerensky cursed a long, low stream of words that I didn't understand. Whether they were Russian or Hebrew or Romanian or all three I don't know. They were involuntary and straight from the bowels of his hatred for the man in front of him.

' . . . Three . . . Four . . . Five . . .'

The Riley Dove flew evenly on. No airpockets or cloud impeded her way through the bright autumn morning.

No further word escaped from Kerensky's throat. His hand moved shuddering across the paper in front of him.

Hartmann lowered the gun.

'A very reasonable and business-like decision, Mr Kerensky,' said Hartmann, turning to point the gun at Joseph.

The other two signed the letter mutely and Hartmann returned it to his briefcase.

'What is his name?' said Hartmann, jerking his head at the unconscious solicitor.

Kerensky told him.

'Good,' said the East German. 'We have specimen signatures of all Smythe's partners and shall compose the necessary standard letter, proving this meeting and countermanding the order to remove the funds to charities.'

He pulled out several more blank sheets of paper, bearing single signatures, and leafed through them. He grunted when he came to a sheet bearing that of the unconscious man. He passed it quickly among the Kerenskys for them to add their signatures.

'We shall type the details above your names later,' he said smiling. 'And that, gentlemen, closes the meeting. Unless there's any other business?'

Kerensky was staring hard at Hartmann. 'How the devil did you get such detailed knowledge of our trust?' He almost shouted the question.

'There is no harm in your knowing now, I suppose,' said Hartmann. His tone was smug. 'Smythe worked for us. He tipped us off about you. You have him to thank for this.'

Kerensky stared in disbelief. His mouth moved but no sound came out. 'But what about the office boy who disappeared?' he asked at last.

'Smythe paid him to disappear,' said Hartmann. 'It was done on our instructions – to fool you, Kerensky.' He paused 'Smythe also worked for the British. Unfortunately for him we discovered this – and that is why we had to kill him.'

Hartmann waited to let this sink in.

'His friend Robson also works for a British intelligence service. He was very wise to withdraw his private help from you. Otherwise we should have had to kill him too. They imagined they had defeated our efforts and closed the trap set by Smythe. They got two of our men at Avignon. But they were wrong.'

Hartmann's eyes bulged until they were visible again in their dark sockets. I realized this happened only when he was angry – or boasting.

'The men they have taken at Avignon know nothing of the scope of our operation. And the British did not imagine we would come back from another direction to complete the programme they kindly worked out for us.' He stopped and looked at his watch.

Kerensky and his brothers remained speechless and immobile in their seats. I had felt Rodica jerk upright behind me as Hartmann mentioned my name.

Hartmann was still looking at his watch. 'Twenty minutes since take-off,' he said in German. 'We should be fifty miles from Jersey now. Just reaching the fringes of the airport's radar coverage.'

131

He walked forward suddenly. 'All right,' he said to the blond German in their own language. 'I'll take over here now. Look after the others.'

He stood slightly behind me looking down over my shoulder.

I gripped the column tightly as I saw the gun in his hand beside my head.

'Take her down – fast!' he snapped in English, knocking the gun against the side of my face.

I flinched and eased the power back. The nose of the Riley Dove began to dip.

'*Die Papiere*,' he called behind him, snapping his fingers. His briefcase was handed to him and he pulled out some more typewritten sheets.

'In a moment I shall hold these papers in front of you, pilot,' he said reverting to English again. 'I want you to read them aloud so that the control tower at Jersey hears clearly. They are the declaration of an emergency. So you will have to act a little. Don't think of disobeying. If you do, the beautiful young lady behind you will be shot.'

We were down below fifteen hundred feet now.

'Put the nose down more steeply,' he ordered, 'and contact Jersey control.'

I did as I was told.

He held a white sheet of paper in front of my nose with two lines typed on it. 'Read it – as if you meant it!' Hartmann ordered.

I opened the radio to the Jersey control tower.

'Mayday! Mayday! Mayday!' I shouted. I tried to disguise my voice from Hartmann. 'This is Golf Alpha Tango Yankee Tango. I have engine failure.' Hartmann had troubled to get the up-to-date jargon for the full call sign, G-ATYT.

The Riley Dove was gathering speed as it rushed downwards. The cream-whipped tops of the waves were clearer now.

'Yankee Tango, this is Jersey approach receiving you. Go ahead.' The calm voice of the controller had an urgent edge to it.

Hartmann turned over the typewritten sheet and pointed to the words on the back.

I read them off into the microphone. 'Jersey approach, this is Yankee Tango. It's the engines! One's already gone; the other's starting to go. It must be the fuel.'

The Riley Dove hurtled downwards.

Hartmann motioned me to switch to receive. 'This is Jersey approach, we acknowledge your message, Yankee Tango. What is your course, height and position please?'

Hartmann held up a new sheet and motioned with the gun for me to read. 'Course two seven zero, about one thousand feet, going down fast. Fifty miles west of Jersey. It must be the wrong fuel! The other engine's packing up now.'

Hartmann had chosen his fictional crisis carefully. A wrongly-refuelled freighter had crashed a few months before. It had taken off all right but when the old fuel in its tanks was burned off the new fuel turned out to be of the wrong density. The freighter had fallen from the sky.

Hartmann turned the paper over. 'Keep going down,' he said calmly.

The Riley Dove was sinking rapidly towards the sea. The altimeter had dropped past seven hundred feet.

I wondered what the hell Hartmann was playing at. Was some Russian submarine going to surface from the Channel to pick them up from life-rafts and leave us threshing around? I tried to concentrate on holding the fast-diving plane and reading the cryptic instructions under my nose. Hartmann rapped his gun on the paper motioning me to read again. 'Three hundred feet now. I can't hold her!' I shouted into the microphone.

He flipped another piece of paper on top of that. 'Two hundred feet. We're going to go in. A hundred feet. Fifty feet. We're going in!'

Hartmann reached out and switched off the radio. I stared ahead through the windscreen. It wouldn't be long before Hartmann's written fiction became fact. Out of the corner of my eye I could see the gun in the East German's hand wavering between the back of my neck and Rodica.

The sea rushed up towards the nose of the Riley Dove.

Twenty-eight

It doesn't take long to travel a hundred feet at over a hundred miles an hour — especially downwards. My instinctive reflexes took over as the Riley Dove flung itself towards the choppy water of the Channel.

I doubt if anybody could be made to commit suicide against his will — even with a gun stuck in his face. So I was easing the stick back before Hartmann gave the order.

'Level out at fifty feet!'

The Riley Dove was already levelling out. The rush of the sea close beneath gave the impression of great acceleration. We swooped down and rose slightly to fly level over the surface at around fifty feet — well below the scan of Jersey's radar.

I imagined the tense expression in the Jersey control tower as our blip disappeared from the screen.

'Fly west for two minutes then turn south,' said Hartmann. He was making sure we cleared the range of the Jersey radar although we were below it. I began to admire the exactness of East Germans' plan and the thoroughness of its execution — now that my heart was thudding less loudly and the adrenalin was on the ebb.

From the corner of my eye I could see beads of sweat standing out on Hartmann's forehead. He had stuck to his orders. A strong German trait. East or West.

I banked the Riley Dove in a wide, gentle turn to the south and the French coast. At fifty feet I didn't want to try to dip the wing steeply. Within a few minutes we came up over Lannion.

'Turn south-east now,' said Hartmann, waving the gun under my nose as we crossed the Brittany coast. 'And start climbing to a normal altitude.'

We climbed towards Rennes. The ascent back into altitudes visible on radar twenty miles from where we 'went in' wouldn't be picked up in Jersey. The air-sea rescue operation would be in full swing by now. It would only be abandoned later when it was decided plane and passengers had disappeared without trace.

But where did we go from here?

When we reached four thousand feet Hartmann ordered me to head due east, mopped his brow with his handkerchief and motioned the other German forward to take over the gun at my head.

I tried to think where we were heading. Hartmann returned to the rear seats and busied himself with more papers from his briefcase, looking frequently at his watch and scribbling on the sheets in front of him.

We were holding a course for Paris. Would we come down somewhere there? The airfield from which the blond pilot had flown Julius's plane earlier perhaps?

I had heard Julius describing to Kerensky what had happened. The East Germans did not attempt to stop the conversation. Julius said he had been forced into the plane in Switzerland on Sunday morning and flown to Paris where he was held prisoner in a hotel room all day with Hartmann. In the mirror I saw Julius darting looks at the blond German as he spoke. They were a mixture of hurt and fury. The German ignored him contemptuously. They had left early this morning to fly to Jersey, Julius said. Hartmann had clearly retreated to Paris from Jersey.

Then another thought struck me – we were heading in a direction that would pick up the international airways across Europe. Our present course would take us over Charlie-Hotel-Whisky, the Chartres beacon south west of Paris. There we could join the routes fanning out all over the Continent. I suddenly sat straighter in my seat. Routes fanning out to West Germany – or even East Germany and the militarily-guarded air corridors to Berlin.

As the outline of the East Germans' plan began to dawn on me, Hartmann spoke in German to the man holding the gun at my head.

'Are you ready to take over the plane in a few minutes?'

'*Ja natürlich*,' he replied.

But to fly across Europe on the airways we needed flight plans and clearances from control tower to control tower. How could the East Germans hope to get across the crowded, commercial air routes without detection?

Then I looked again in the mirror at the frown of concentration on Hartmann's face as he bent over his papers in the rear of the plane. His blond helper was getting ready to take the controls. Perhaps he had already filed a flight plan under different registration letters from somewhere. Were we about to change our identity as well as our route?

I realized I needed to stay in control of the plane if we were to stand any chance of preventing the East Germans hijacking the Kerensky Trust – and me. Once I was out of the driving seat I would probably be recognized. And then what? I remembered Hartmann's earlier reference to Clarence Smythe and me. I looked again in the mirror and saw the ashen, unconscious face of the solicitor. The blood on his head wound had congealed now.

In a few minutes I would be ordered from the controls. Where was the Errol Flynn inspiration now that I needed it?

We were south of Dinard, at about five thousand feet when I saw the inspiration. It was coming in from the north-east above and to the left of us. A BAC1–11 charter heading down to land at Dinard. It went by a mile away and a thousand feet higher. The gunman at my side didn't notice it because of the conversation with Hartmann in the rear of the plane. I climbed steadily and headed north-east to cut the track of the jet that was now going down behind us into Dinard.

I was wondering whether I had misjudged when a short sharp bump rocked the nose of the Riley Dove. It swung left. The controls jerked in my hand and I wondered whether I had been wise. Then the whole plane rocked, shuddered and dropped. The blond German clutched at my seat with his free hand to keep his balance. He could see me fighting the controls.

The uneven flight continued for a moment. Then the plane swung violently, the left wing dipped and fell past the vertical. My seat belt held me but the vast German at my side tumbled heavily against the side of the fuselage. I tried to correct with the controls but nothing happened.

The horizon twisted and swung crazily and the Riley Dove

roared wildly out of control in the wake turbulence of the jetliner into which I had deliberately headed.

When we stopped falling I levelled out with shaking hands. The altimeter showed that we'd dropped four hundred feet.

'I'd only read about wake turbulence before. The advent of Jumbo jets had prompted new research into why wing tips left a wake of twisted, horizontal tornadoes that can hang around in the air for up to half an hour. Now I knew how dangerous they were at first hand.

I had meant to grab the gun from the German and try to put him out of action during the wake turbulence confusion. I looked down at him. The gun had fallen from his hand and he was lying still on the floor. His neck was twisted at an odd angle. He was the only one in the plane not strapped into his seat when we hit the jet's slipstream.

Hartmann hurried forward, gun in hand and knelt by the fallen man. He ordered Joseph Croissé to help him get him upright and they dragged him to a rear seat. Croissé snivelled and helped without defiance. But the blond pilot did not open his eyes. His face was pallid. I guessed and hoped that he had broken his neck when the plane went out of control.

Hartmann came back in a furious rage. '*Du verdammter Schweinhund!*' His face twisted as he spat out his German equivalent of four-letter words. He just managed to prevent himself doing a similar injury to me. But he couldn't fly the plane on his own. He stood by me breathing heavily – trying to control his anger. Hartmann had obviously read about wake turbulence too.

'You flew into the trail of that jet deliberately,' he shouted in English. 'You could have killed us all! I may kill you for that, pilot, when we get where we are going!'

'And where's that, Hartmann?' I asked, not bothering to disguise my voice. I was indispensable – conscious – now.

He reached out and snatched the headset and hat off. Then he pulled the gold-rimmed spectacles roughly from my eyes. 'Robson! Mr Robson, master of disguises,' said Hartmann theatrically. 'Refuser of good advice to go home.'

He did a quick search of my clothes and hauled the Webley & Scott revolver from my waistband.

He slapped my face suddenly with his open left hand and the plane banked momentarily as I recoiled. He glared down at me. 'Wait until we get down on the ground in the DDR, Robson,' he said in a barely audible voice.

'So that's where we're going,' I said brightly. 'But we haven't got visas. And we haven't got flight plans and clearance across several NATO countries. Maybe they will send up fighters to shoot you down, Hartmann.'

He resisted the taunts and stared at me in silence. 'You will do exactly as I say, Robson, or the girl behind you and everybody else in the plane will be shot one by one. And you last of all.'

I looked up at him but his eyes were no longer visible in the deep sockets.

'And we have a perfectly workable plan to fly through the powerful countries of NATO without harm.' He jabbed the point of the barrel roughly into my neck. 'Without harm to me, that is.'

'What are you going to do with us, Hartmann, in East Germany?' I asked.

'You will be our guests, or the guests of Moscow, perhaps.'

'Do you think the British and French governments will accept that without protest?' I said. 'You may be interested to know Hartmann, that I wrote the whole story of this escapade and posted it to a Fleet Street paper today. To be opened if I don't phone them by tonight.'

'That's melodramatic nonsense, Robson, and you know it,' he said briskly. 'We shall announce that you and the Kerenskys have defected. That you faked a crash into the sea and a false story in order to cover your tracks. "Defectors go East!" It will be a big scandal, your defection. We shall denounce your Fleet Street story in our press as a smoke screen thrown up by your intelligence organs. Can anybody prove the Trust exists now?'

The three Kerenskys were visible in my mirror. They sat listlessly, strapped in their seats. George Kerensky occasionally passed a hand fretfully over his face. I realized I hadn't seen Rodica since we took off.

'Rodica, are you all right?' I asked over my shoulder.

'Yes,' she said quickly, 'don't worry about me.'

'Shut up,' shouted Hartmann. Then he lowered his voice. 'So we are on first-name terms, are we? I see you in a new gallant light, Robson. Who would have thought . . . ?'

Hartmann's heavy joke was interrupted by the radio. 'Paris Control to unidentified aircraft twenty-five miles due west Charlie-Hotel-Whisky. Identify yourself please.'

The voice of the Paris controller came clearly into the cabin. Hartmann had disconnected the headset when he pulled off my cap.

'Wait,' shouted Hartmann and hurried to the back of the plane. He returned with his briefcase and took out more typewritten sheets. He scribbled in an addition. Then he plugged the headset in and held it in his hand with the microphone in front of me.

'Read as instructed,' he said, pushing the top one under my nose.

I read from the paper. 'Paris Control, I am Hawker Siddeley Dove freighter, Golf Alpha Delta Papa Golf, twenty-five miles west of Chartres, at five thousand feet.' Hartmann had changed us to a Dove transport, registration G-ADPG.

The Paris controller wasn't satisfied with that. 'Papa Golf, where are you heading please?'

I read again. 'Paris Control, Papa Golf is bound Würzburg, West Germany. We have filed flight plan from La Baule, Brittany to route along airways Chartres-Paris, Paris-Luxembourg, Luxembourg-Frankfurt-am-Main.'

There was a long pause.

Then we heard the controller swearing softly to himself and his colleagues. '*Merde, alors*, here's another one with no flight plan.' To us he said, 'Papa Golf, Paris Control has no flight plan for you, did you file one?'

I looked at the next line. Hartmann had done his homework well. 'Paris Control, that is nothing new in experience of Papa Golf. Flight plans go astray more often than virgins these days.

If you're stuck I'll give it to you over the air. It will probably turn up after we've gone.'

Hartmann's organization knew something about the overworked French traffic controllers. I felt him tense beside me as his bluff was put to the test. He knew his theory was good but would the Paris controller accept us without a plan, or try to turn us back to La Baule?

After another longer silence Paris Control came back 'Papa Golf, give me your details. I will clear you.'

Hartmann pulled away the top paper with a smirk of self-satisfaction spreading over his face. Underneath, a flight plan had been filled out with details from La Baule to Würzburg. I read them over.

As I waited for the reply I noticed the typed sheets were headed with a German name – presumably that of the pilot with the broken neck who should have been flying the plane by now. At least I'd made a slight dent in their plans.

The radio crackled again. 'Paris Control, Papa Golf. Take Red Six Chartres-Paris, Blue Nine Paris-Luxembourg and Amber Sixteen Luxembourg-Frankfurt.'

Another typewritten sheet appeared in front of me. 'Roger. Papa Golf thanks Paris Control for its kindness. And wishes you as much luck with the virgins.' I winced at Hartmann's idea of English repartee.

I felt Hartmann relax slightly beside me as we flew on into Red Six over the Chartres beacon heading for the French capital.

The Riley Dove had a range of over a thousand miles. There seemed to be nothing to stop us now between Paris and the East German border fifty miles north-east of Würzburg.

I reflected on what Rodica had said earlier. A hundred and fifty thousand pounds was no use to a dead man. It was no use to a man held behind the Iron Curtain either. And it was certainly no use if the source of the money was also flying steadily towards the Iron Curtain at a hundred and eighty miles an hour at a cruising altitude of six thousand feet.

Twenty-nine

The Riley Dove flew on peacefully for two hours although it had a man with a gun in its nose instead of an olive branch.

Hartmann stood stolidly beside me as we cruised through Red Six, climbed into Blue Nine after Paris then switched to Amber Sixteen over Luxembourg. The approval of the controller at Paris had been passed down. Hartmann had further scripts ready for me to read when we called the Luxembourg and Frankfurt towers. But they didn't query us, just handed us on eastwards.

Some cloud was beginning to blow like fluff across the face of the sunny afternoon. It was after three o'clock when we changed our north-easterly course to pass south of Frankfurt in the direction of Würzburg.

Frankfurt lies about seventy-five miles west of the fortified frontier of East Germany. Würzburg to the south-east is about fifty miles short of it. Our heading now was taking us on a slowly converging parallel course with the East German border. But some time we would have to break abruptly northwards towards Communist territory. Otherwise we should fly on south of Hartmann's homeland altogether towards Austria. That was the moment we would look suspicious. I hoped somebody would notice this on a radar screen.

'I wonder if some bright traffic controller has looked up your false "Golf Alpha Delta Papa Golf" registration and found it's a Tiger Moth in the Outer Hebrides,' I said to Hartmann.

'Shut up, Robson,' he said. 'You are a fool. Like everything else, that has been carefully checked. The letters are in fact those of a grounded Dove Transport. It is kept at Bournemouth and all this week is undergoing a maintenance check at a small airfield. It is owned by the Trelawny Charter Company, and that is who you are if any tower asks.'

The dark holes in his face seemed to deepen. I supposed he was smiling at his own cleverness.

The Kerenskys and Rodica had sat silent in their straps since Chartres seemingly stunned by the realization that their nightmare was drawing towards a climax.

'Why must you take us with you?' blurted Joseph Croissé suddenly. He was sitting on one of the facing seats with his back to us. He spoke over his shoulder. 'You have all our money. We are no use to you. Let us go.'

Hartmann turned towards the speaker. 'That, I should have thought, was obvious,' he said slowly. 'Do you think I'm going to risk leaving you free to nullify the arrangements with the Zurich bank? So that Hartmann Investments doesn't get what you – by your "Discretionary Powers" – have decided to award them? No, my friends. Our plan compels us to keep you out of circulation. It would have been simpler perhaps to kill you.' Hartmann's voice was coolly matter-of-fact. 'But we needed to get home quickly and safely – and it was more convenient to use your transport. It is as simple as that. We prefer not to take life unless we have to, of course.' He had adopted a tone of mock affability. 'You will be guests behind the dreaded "Iron Curtain". What will happen to you eventually will be decided not by me, but by others. In addition we have plans for operations in other tax havens which your knowledge might jeopardize.'

Then he lost interest in the subject. He looked at his watch and checked the compass. 'Change your heading and fly north-east!' he commanded, suddenly digging the pistol in my neck for emphasis.

We were twenty-five miles short of Würzburg. I swung the nose of the Riley Dove towards the East German border. It was about forty-five miles away, straight ahead – fifteen to twenty minutes' flying time at our present speed.

'Open up the throttles,' Hartmann commanded. 'I want to get home fast; I am tired of your company.'

I did as I was told and headed for a life under Communism at about two hundred miles an hour.

It would be less than fifteen minutes now.

I had toured the East German border with a party of journalists from Berlin several years before. We'd visited German and American bases, where keen eyes kept a constant watch on the border air space. I guessed that our sudden turn and dash for the frontier would be registering now on flickering radar screens. I looked out through the side windows for some flash of silver that would mean a NATO fighter coming up to look at us and lend a hand.

But five minutes passed without anything happening.

Then the radio crackled. 'Frankfurt tower to Papa Golf. Papa Golf, you have changed your heading. You are now flying directly towards East German border, not Würzburg. Please make course correction and advise.'

I looked expectantly towards Hartmann. He said nothing but leaned forward to hold the switch on the boom microphone in the 'off' position so there could be no reply.

'Frankfurt tower to Papa Golf. Papa Golf, please acknowledge . . .'

Hartmann turned down the volume of the Frankfurt controller.

'Open the throttles right up,' he ordered. And jabbed the gun in my neck again.

I pushed the Riley Dove to its maximum for the height and we sped on at two hundred and fifty miles an hour towards East Germany.

When we were about three minutes from the border I saw two Starfighters with the markings of the Bundesrepublik rising fast on our left from the Fulda area. They were a bit late. The NATO radar plotters had been very slow getting them off the ground. But then I suppose they were more concerned with watching for unidentified flying objects coming *out* of the East.

Hartmann saw them at the same moment and leaned forward to peer out through the screen.

As he did so I took the chance to swing the nose of the Riley Dove a few degrees eastwards. We were approaching East Germany where the border, after running south for three hundred miles from the Baltic, makes a ninety-degree turn east. At this point I knew an udder-like projection of East Germany hung down narrow-necked into the Western world.

'Frankfurt tower to Papa Golf, repeat, please acknowledge . . .' The radio headset hanging on its hook still carried the voice of the Frankfurt tower controller quietly on low volume as the Starfighters closed up fast on us from below.

'Dive!'

Hartmann uttered the word sharply. He encouraged me with another dig in the side of the neck. The spot was getting sore.

The Riley Dove seemed to be standing still against the quicksilver ripple of the Starfighters. They flashed upwards through the straggling, clotted lints of clouds like small fish darting among the reeds of a river. They were climbing in a fast, shallow curve. I could see the flared black-cross-on-white markings of the West German *Bundeswehr* under the canopy and on the wings as the first jet interceptor shot smoothly upwards. It was an F 104G, which I knew was capable of about 1500 m.p.h.

By the time they reached the height we had been flying at we were nearly a thousand feet lower, and still diving. The high speed of the jets took them several miles above us before they could turn and bank down again. The Riley Dove lumbered in comparison, but it didn't need so much room to change its manoeuvre.

'Papa Golf. . .Papa Golf, please acknowledge, plea . . .' The barely audible voice from Frankfurt was cut completely as Hartmann leaned forward and switched to a new frequency.

The radio crackled afresh. Then a new voice came on talking to us – this time in German.

'Erfurt Control tower to Papa Golf. Do you read us, Hartmann? You seem to be right on schedule.' Erfurt had obviously been listening to Frankfurt.

The voice, I realized, was coming from inside East Germany. At the same moment I looked down and caught my first glimpse of the border directly ahead.

Ugly wooden towers and high, wire fences. A mile-wide mined strip of no-man's-land scarring the green forest of Thuringia. Broken X shapes of iron girder and cement tank traps. Barbed-wire entanglements.

Hartmann gave a grunt of satisfaction as he saw it. And continued to hold the gun behind my head.

The fortified border passed underneath, slipped behind and we flew on into East Germany, still losing height.

'Welcome to the DDR, Robson,' he said in English and laughed shortly. Over his shoulder he said, 'The DDR extends a warm welcome to three distinguished ex-millionaires.'

The Kerenskys stared down numbly through the windows.

'Erfurt control to Papa Golf. Do you read us, Hartmann?' The East German voice repeated its demand.'

Hartmann reached forward for the boom microphone and headset, and switched it to transmit.

'Erfurt Control, this is Papa Golf, this is Papa Golf. Hartmann speaking. I am bringing the goods home on schedule.'

The thwarted Starfighters who started too late were climbing high into the sky behind now, holding off from the border. They probably saw the Russian-built MiG 19s rising ahead of us before I did. The Starfighters were pulling back to avoid an armed clash.

The foolish private plane that had strayed over the border into Communist territory was on its own now. They were climbing higher to watch but not advancing any more to try to impede or help.

Thirty

The gloating expression etched on Hartmann's face gave a new brightness to the black sockets under his jutting brow. He went to switch the radio to receive, then changed his mind and spoke again.

'Erfurt Control, Papa Golf. You can call off the MiG watchdogs. Everything is under control. I can bring them in alone.' Then he leaned forward expectantly, waiting for more praise.

We had levelled out now at around three thousand feet. Lumpy cloud still obscured the ground from time to time. The sun was shining directly behind, reminding us that it would soon be sinking in the West while we were sinking in the East.

'Papa Golf, Erfurt Control, you are heading too far south, please correct . . .'

The next words were drowned by Rodica shouting behind me. 'For God's sake somebody do something before it's too late.'

Hartmann swung furiously on her, waving the gun in her face. 'Shut up!'

I leaned forward in the same instant to switch off the radio. Hartmann turned back.

'Keep still, Rodica,' I shouted. Hartmann cuffed me with the barrel of the pistol. The Riley Dove reared but I righted it.

He leaned back to the radio and switched on. 'Erfurt Control, please repeat . . .'

'The briefcase,' I shouted over my shoulder to Rodica, 'I need my briefcase.'

Hartmann was still straining for the voice from Erfurt. 'Keep still,' he snapped, waving his gun sideways.

I heard Rodica fumble with the box and string. Hartmann looked round.

He shied back suddenly, throwing up his arms as the first bat fluttered erratically up from beside Rodica's seat. It crashed around inside the cockpit, knocking against the glass of the windscreen. It screeched its tiny, piping cries as it flew blindly in the cabin of the diving aircraft. Hartmann was swiping wildly at the bat with his gun hand when the second one rose from the box, screaming its almost inaudible screams of fright after several hours confined.

Perhaps the bats sensed the German's irrational, exaggerated fear. The second one fluttered fast and unerring to the side of its mate, swooping and crying around Hartmann's bobbing head.

I flung the stick forward and dipped the right wing into a steep, turning dive.

The voice from Erfurt came through the headset which had fallen by my feet. Again it demanded a course correction. 'Papa Golf, you are too far south! Papa Golf, are you receiving me? Please acknowledge.'

The radio continued to crackle and splutter with German words as the Riley Dove headed down into a solid lump of cloud that cut out the sun and let only a fogged light through the windscreen.

Hartmann lunged hysterically at the bats, ducking and flinching as they flitted around him. He had half fallen as I put the nose into a dive. One of the bats crashed against the windscreen and fell beside Hartmann's head. He twisted upright and slammed the butt of his gun down on the tiny, mouselike body. There was a squelching sound. Hartmann uttered muffled curses as the gun

146

butt rose and fell, pulping the bat's body into a shapeless mess on the floor of the cabin.

His body heaved and shook as he concentrated all his attention on destroying the tiny animal responsible for his shaming fear.

I reached forward and twisted the master knob of the radio. I wrenched it violently against its thread and broke it off putting the set out of action. I wondered if I could leave my seat long enough to kick Hartmann senseless as he crawled around on the floor after the bats. But the Riley Dove was still tobogganing downwards through the thick cloud.

Hartmann scrambled after the second bat. He smashed his gun against the side of the plane catching it a glancing blow and pinning it by a wing. It fell. He rained blows at it on the floor, squashing it into a soup of blood and tissues. Finally he heaved himself upright and crushed the remains beneath his heel.

He rushed forward down the sloping plane. He was panting and his chest heaved from the exertion. He looked down at me wild-eyed.

He fought down an impulse to crush my head to pulp like the bats, and spat curses in German instead. He grabbed the seat to steady himself as we continued diving.

We came out of the cloud at about eight hundred feet. To my dismay the sun still shone from behind us. We were still heading east. The runway appeared suddenly among the pines of the Thuringian forest two miles in front of the Riley Dove's dipping nose.

The gun went back to the sore inflamed hole in my neck.

'All right, Robson. Take it down carefully – or I might kill you before we hit the ground.'

I got the flaps and landing gear down and eased back the power.

The aircraft built for business executives floated forwards and downwards at about ninety knots, with its cargo of three frightened millionaires, an unconscious solicitor, a blond German with a broken neck, a girl who looked like a beautiful frightened nun, an East German gunman who hated bats – and a pilot with a gun at his head who was dreading touching down on an East German runway.

My landing was messy. I hit the ground and bounced up again. Hit it a second time and held. I braked and slowed the Riley Dove.

A jumble of buildings stood at the end of the runway. As we slowed to fifty knots I shouted over my shoulder, 'Keep your seat belts fastened everybody! I might try to get off the ground again!'

The gun in Hartmann's hand exploded. The noise deafened me. He had fired it two feet from my left ear.

It exploded again. The second bullet smashed through the instrument panel shattering the magneto switches. The first one had smashed into the bottom of the control column. He fired a third shot at the column.

I was surprised for a moment that the bullets were not fired at me.

Then the plane began swinging and bucking. I realized Hartmann had deliberately tried to disable it, to ground it finally.

I forced all my weight down on the brakes as we slewed sideways. The Riley Dove ran off the runway and veered across the grass, trying to overturn. One wing buried itself in a lightly constructed weather hut a hundred and fifty yards from the runway.

We shuddered to a halt.

Hartmann flung open the door. A group of men were running from the jumble of buildings. A yellow fire truck was starting towards us. Hartmann still had the gun in his hand. He waved his other hand in greeting at the running men.

Then he stiffened. I looked past him over his shoulder to where he was looking. And saw the airfield sign on top of a hangar.

Coburg!

I *had* got the Riley Dove across that narrow, five-mile neck of the bulbous udder of East Germany that hangs southward. My rough navigation while Hartmann was preoccupied with first the Starfighters, then the bats, had worked. Coburg lies in the jetty of West German land that juts into the East alongside the udder of Communist territory. We had crossed back over the border in the cloud.

Hartmann finished working that out at the same time as I did. I was fumbling to free the buckle of my seat belt. Hartmann looked round frantically. He had realized the ultimate irony. He had trapped himself by disabling the plane. He started to turn back from the doorway.

I freed the belt and lunged from my seat, cannoning against him. My hunched shoulder caught him low down. He twisted, fell backwards out of the door of the Riley Dove and landed heavily on the ground. The gun spun away into the grass.

I jumped through the door and pinned him to the ground.

The group of running men arrived and started shouting questions in German. A blue car with the official police crest of the German Federal Republic on its side raced out from the airfield buildings. Two uniformed West German police carrying short, automatic rifles on slings over their shoulders hurried over.

'Look after him,' I said, getting off the winded Hartmann. 'And keep a very close eye on him. He's a VIP from the East. He's decided to defect.'

They looked dubious but moved in and handcuffed him anyway.

I heard the two West German Starfighters sweeping in from the West having rounded the Communist border. They were still searching to finish their reports. They peeled off and came back low over Coburg airfield in a fast run to have another look. I glanced up northwards towards the border. There was no sign of the Russian-built MiGs. Like the Starfighters earlier they were wisely holding back behind the cloud on their side of the frontier.

I turned back to the Riley Dove. Rodica was a purple and grey figure in the doorway looking out. The Kerensky brothers crowded behind her. They still didn't really know where they were. I moved forward to help them down.

I assumed the polite expression of an airline employee. 'Welcome to Coburg, West Germany,' I said. 'I hope you enjoyed your flight.'

Thirty-one

Rodica swung.

The number seven iron flew through a perfect arc. There was a clean, crisp 'thwock' as she connected. I gazed in open-mouthed admiration. Her tall, taut body held the pose, her copper hair streamed down her back. Her chin was tilted, her arms held aloft and the thick white sweater pulled itself elegantly tight around her, following the swing and swell of her hips.

'You're supposed to watch the ball,' she said out of the side of her mouth, still looking ahead and holding the pose.

I turned reluctantly away in time to see the tiny white ball bounce and roll on to the green of the short first hole at La Moye. Another golfer walking by looking over his shoulder to study the finer points of Rodica's fluid, supple swing, stepped straight into a bunker, dragging his trolley and clubs behind him. He smiled foolishly at us, dug himself out and walked on. Still casting looks back at Rodica.

The tide was out in St Ouen's Bay below the cliff-top golf course. Planes rose regularly from Jersey Airport a mile away, crossed the jumble of runway light poles, set like metallic sunflowers in the cliff-face, and headed out westwards.

'As one tax-avoider to another, I think I might congratulate you on a perfect shot, Miss Kerensky,' I said.

We had called at the bank on the way to the course and I had opened my Jersey account with the Kerensky cheque.

'Call me George, Jonathan,' Kerensky had said as he handed it over.

The flight back from Coburg to Jersey in a newly-chartered aircraft with a professional pilot had been uneventful. There had been a routine annual meeting of the Kerensky Trust over the Channel as the plane crossed from France towards Jersey. Letters awarding twenty-five million pounds to Hartmann Investments of Liechtenstein were torn up and the accounts were read in full. A solicitor, with a bandaged head and looking not at all well, had witnessed some signatures. Various sums were distributed to various companies. The meeting was over before the plane flew into Jersey at a few minutes to midnight. The Trust members had come close to their deadline for the meeting but they had met it.

There had been a delay of about three hours before we were able to get away from Coburg.

The British Embassy in Paris had at first insisted on the telephone that there was *nobody* by the name of Carruthers on their staff. But at last, after a demand that everybody in the Embassy be told that a Mr Robson was calling him, the rounded vowels of a man did come on the line and admit he had at some time been referred to as Carruthers. He was told a Mr Hartmann was waiting to talk to him at Coburg and he flew down immediately in a private plane.

There had been a lot of tedious questions in Coburg. Then Carruthers had arrived. He had walked up to a pilot in a blue uniform and gold-rimmed spectacles in the airport buildings and asked where he could find a Mr Robson. And the pilot had removed his cap and told Carruthers that he had found him. In a Bavarian accent.

Carruthers hadn't laughed.

He had just looked faintly exasperated. As if he'd been got out of bed unexpectedly after a bout of stomach trouble.

Carruthers had used his commanding tones with all the uniformed and civilian men who seemed closely interested in Mr Hartmann. Carruthers's manner showed he was the most closely interested of all. He looked as if he could hardly wait for interrogation to begin. Ask him particularly if it was to have been a financial offensive, the pilot said. Carruthers scowled. There was to be nothing in the press.

The pilot in the blue uniform called a Fleet Street number and asked an editor not to open a letter addressed to him. Carruthers called Jersey CID and spoke soothingly to them.

Rodica Kerensky refused to speak to the pilot in the blue uniform and gold-rimmed spectacles, tossing her head angrily and saying he had been working for certain organizations all the time and had deceived her and her father.

The pilot eventually asked Carruthers to describe to Miss Kerensky how he had tried to prevent the pilot returning to Jersey from St Malo and – to the pilot's surprise – he did it very

151

accurately. But he still didn't smile or laugh. In fact he confided to Miss Kerensky that he would be very pleased to see Mr Robson return to Jersey as soon as possible. And remain there.

Then there had been the uneventful flight home. Uneventful of course apart from that little piece of business. It might have seemed unusual to those not used to handling large sums of money. But to those who were? No.

There was a body in the pilot's bed when he got back to the fortified farmhouse in Jersey. A live one. It sat up blinking as he switched on the light. 'I've been waiting for you to come for a long time, Jonathan,' said the tousled dark head, pouting. The sheets slipped from a careless fist revealing that the body was not only live, but naked.

The pilot fled.

He took a taxi to the Grand Hotel on the Esplanade at St Helier, apologized for not having paid an earlier bill and booked in for the night. With the protection of daylight he returned to the farmhouse without the pilot's uniform.

I struck my third shot into a bunker by the first green and hurried after Rodica.

'Venetian marble,' I asked as I caught her up, 'you think that might be a good investment, do you? A good hedge against inflation for the medium-term investor . . . ?'

ANTHONY GREY

Tokyo Bay

£6.99

Pearl Harbor, Nagasaki, Hiroshima . . . the greatest East–West conflagrations in history. But where did the terrible mistrust which sparked these cataclysms spring from?

Vital clues emerge from the dramatic events of July 1853 when steam-driven US Navy warships loomed shockingly out of the haze cloaking Tokyo Bay. Rumours that foreign monsters had arrived on smoking volcanoes engulfed the civilian population in hysteria – and hordes of feudal warriors rushed to defend the coastline of the world's most isolated realm.

TOKYO BAY

With these two nations teetering on the brink of war, Robert Eden, an idealistic young New England officer, swims secretly ashore on his own unauthorized peace mission, inspired by the haunting moonlit beacon of Mount Fuji.

On land he clashes with fearsome sword-wielding samurai led by the formidable Prince Tanaka Yoshio – and encounters Tokiwa, a beautiful and courageous geisha fleeing amidst the general panic. The intense emotional entanglements that follow will ensnare Eden and his descendants in Japan's destiny for generations to come.

With this enthralling first novel of a new Asian trilogy, the author of worldwide bestsellers SAIGON and PEKING illuminates as never before a little-known historical episode which helped shape the modern world.

ANTHONY GREY

Saigon

£6.99

Joseph Sherman first saw Saigon in 1925, a wide-eyed fifteen-year-old on a hunting expedition with his family. Through five decades, he returned again and again, drawn back as much by the strange and magical land as by Lan, the Vietnamese beauty he could never forget.

He was there when the hatred of a million coolies rose against the French, and he was there when the Legion fought its last and bloody stand at Dien Bien Phu.

He saw military 'advisers' fire their first shots in America's hopeless war against the blood-red tide of revolution, and he climbed aboard one of the last US helicopters as they fled the fallen city of Saigon.

'An absorbing saga . . . an epic novel. Anthony Grey is not just a man of steely courage as his survival through two years in a Peking prison demonstrated. He is one of that rare species – a born storyteller'
Daily Mail

'Does for the Vietnam Wars what Leo Tolstoy did for the Napoleonic Wars . . . Indeed this masterwork could well be called the *War and Peace* of our age'
San Francisco Chronicle

ANTHONY GREY

Peking

£6.99

To a China racked by famine and bloody civil war a young English-born missionary brings all the crusading passion of his untried Christian faith. He burns to save the world's largest nation from Communism.

But on the Long March, amidst horror and despair too great for Christianity to salve, Jakob Kellner becomes entangled with Mei-ling, a beautiful and fervent revolutionary. Powerful new emotions challenge and reshape his faith – and entrap him for life in that vast country's tortured destiny.

With PEKING Anthony Grey, the bestselling author of SAIGON, enshrines in towering fiction the turbulent half-century of conflict, struggle and idealism which marked China's revolution.

From the heroic and self-sacrificing Long March of the 1930s to the human suffering at the core of the recent Cultural Revolution, this epic masterpiece brilliantly illuminates the grandeur of China's past – and present. To read PEKING is to begin to understand modern China.

'Gripping fiction . . . part epic, part blockbuster'
The Times

'An excellent read, panoramic in scope and often powerful in effect . . . Fascinating stuff: but what lingers on is the teller of the tale, the voice behind it'
Financial Times

ANTHONY GREY

The Chinese Assassin

£5.99

When an airliner crashes in Mongolia the Chinese government keep suspiciously quiet regarding its contents. Yet a year later they claim one of the victims was Lin Piao, Chinese Defence Minister, fleeing to Russia after an abortive attempt to assassinate Mao and seize power. How did Lin Piao die? Was it an accident or was it murder? As the secret services of Russia, China and America clash, the most destructive earthquake since the fifteenth century rocks China, and the dying Mao comes face to face with a deadly assassin.

'Chillingly authentic'
Yorkshire Post

ANTHONY GREY

The Bangkok Secret

£5.99

A 40-year-old unsolved murder in the Royal Palace of Bangkok – the search in the jungles of Thailand for a missing father who holds the key to . . .

THE BANGKOK SECRET

Joceline Hampson, internationally acclaimed TV journalist; a woman whose quest for the inside story of Thailand's King Rama VIII leads her into a desperate world of mystery and intrigue.

Hidden among the spirit-worshipping tribes and the heroin smugglers of the Golden Triangle she seeks clues to the brutal murder of a young king – and the last people to see her father alive . . .

But in the midst of her courageous mission lies the unseen danger of one more violent death – her own . . .

'Anthony Grey is one of that rare species – a born storyteller'
Daily Mail

ANTHONY GREY

The Bulgarian Exclusive

£5.99

'Why Robson, Comrade?'

'Because he knows Eastern Europe well. He also has an almost psychotic hatred of everything communist . . . He is not beyond foolhardy actions and he has shown himself to have a very low resistance threshold to attractive women.'

An assignment in Sofia turns into an extremely rocky ride for BAPPA reporter Jonathan Robson, sent to cover the Bulgarian Communist Party Congress. Journalist or spy? Many would like to know the answer. Asking 'unnecessary' questions has always been Robson's stock in trade . . .

But this time he could be in way over his head.

'This hard-hitting tale asks to be read at one sitting'
Yorkshire Post

'A real cliffhanger . . . Grey makes the story too real for comfort, the Bulgarian atmosphere very authentic'
Publishers Weekly

ANTHONY GREY

The Naked Angels

£5.99

They're women prepared to go to any lengths to save the planet from destruction.

'So no provision had been made?' asked Conroy.

Garstenmeyer drew himself up to his full height – five feet four inches. 'No specific provision has been made against the ground opening up and swallowing the President, no, sir,' he replied . . .

The Cold War is over. Almost overnight the two most powerful enemies in the world become friends. But did this earth-shaking happening take place before or after the President of the United States' sudden disappearance in Berlin? Or during?

And did it really take the most sexually alluring woman in all of human history to make him change his mind? A woman who was prepared to do the same – if necessary – to another desperate, ageing male in Moscow?

Anthony Grey's novel is the first gripping account of one of diplomacy's best-kept secrets – the mystery-shrouded deeds of THE NAKED ANGELS . . .

'Anthony Grey is one of that rare species – a born storyteller'
Daily Mail